Make do and Mend

MURIEL CLARK

With Best Wishes

from

Muriel Clark.

COLLINS
Glasgow and London

First published 1978
Published by William Collins Sons and Company Limited

Copyright © 1978 Muriel Clark

Printed in Great Britain

ISBN 0 00 434612 2

CONTENTS

chapter 1

SPENDING

We live in a consumer society which is consuming too much too quickly. This is an age of take-away and throw-away; obsolescence is planned and instant products abound. Consequently, individual ingenuity and practical creativity are at a low ebb. Daily we are confronted with the pressures to buy, to have now and pay later. There is little incentive to be content with less or to make do with simpler alternatives. But in all the rush and struggle to earn money to pay bills and acquire possessions, we put at risk much more important things – health, peace of mind, time for family and friends. We need to relax, calm down and adopt a more 'anti-consumer' attitude.

The inescapable fact remains, however, that everything in life must be paid for. The payment may be in terms of cash, time or effort – mental or physical. These three exist in a tripartite balance, and cutting down on one means expending more on the others. For example, less money coming in means that more time and effort must be spent in the economic running of the home. On the other hand, a career woman may have more money but she will certainly have less time, so this must be bought in the form of extra help or labour-saving aids. It could prove cheaper for a working wife to give up her job. The economies which can be made in the home, given the time, are often underestimated, and by the time these savings are added to the cost of transport, clothes, make-up and hairdos, the total may not fall far short of the earnings sacrificed. People work for reasons other than money, of course, but the pleasure of being master of your own time seems to be vanishing in a rising sense of inadequacy if one does not go out to work. Never lose sight of the fact that when time becomes master of *you* this is an unsatisfactory state of affairs leading to neither health nor happiness.

Money is nothing in itself, yet it determines almost everything in our lives. Think of money mainly in terms of the things it can do for you, then sort these into an order of priority. It is not always easy to establish priorities, and people who cannot see beyond the next pay packet are bound to run into difficulties, since bills do not present themselves in the same orderly sequence as pay. One large item of expenditure may demand the whole of the weekly or monthly income, whereupon the lack of any system becomes quite apparent to the unfortunate person who has founded his or her economy on hope.

Why bother to live within your means? Some people rely on the benevolent state to provide whenever they fail to cope by themselves. State provision is useful but minimal, as those who manage to get by on pensions and allowances readily admit, and it merely changes one set of problems for another. Being poor is hard work, but hard work alone never killed anyone, and there *is* a sense of achievement in being master of your resources. Oddly enough, it can be a greater sense of achievement (though you may doubt!) than bringing home a large pay packet and wondering how to spend the surplus.

Few people manage to live happily in a state of constant financial distress – most of us worry and fret about paying bills and coping with emergencies. If you can get your finances under control so that needless worry is eliminated as far as possible, you will be both happier and healthier. Most doctors agree that many of today's ailments are due to stress and worry, so by reducing them you can improve the quality of your life. Some of the economies suggested in this book will present a challenge; choose from amongst them, and you may also find a bonus in a new interest or hobby.

Needs and wants

Some expenses are essential for survival, others are not, so spending can be conveniently grouped into needs and wants which, since they are not the same for everyone, must be considered in relation to individual circumstances.

Priority needs

These are common to us all, and money must be allocated to them before all else. Man does not live by bread alone; on the other hand he certainly does not live long without it, so food is a top priority, along with shelter (which means rent or mortgage and rates) and warmth in the form of fuel and clothing. There is some element of choice within these areas, for example in the type of house you live in, the sort of food you buy, the way you heat your home and how you are clothed. It is vitally important that you are properly fed (which does not necessarily mean expensively fed) and that your living conditions are warm and reasonably comfortable. Health comes before everything else, so do not scrimp on food and fuel in order to buy less necessary luxuries.

Other needs

The next consideration is personal needs – a flautist needs a flute! Many people have to provide themselves with the tools of their trade – equipment, books, protective or fashionable clothing, instruments and tools. Remember that these expenses can be claimed from the Inland Revenue when filling in your annual income tax return form.

Travel to work in order to earn money is necessary for most people and this must be paid for. A car may become necessary when there is no public transport. If the expense of buying and running a car is just too much to bear, other possibilities must be considered. How far from work do you live? Would it be possible to get there on two wheels – motor cycle, scooter or pedal-pusher? The last is obviously cheapest, it is also very good exercise, and, in an urban area, frequently quicker than travelling by car. Three-wheeled is cheaper than four-wheeled transport to tax and insure. Or perhaps you could share transport and costs with someone else travelling in the same direction. Walking is the forgotten art – but it may serve to take you the length of public transport or a lift. If none of these suggestions proves feasible, it is worth considering a move nearer to work, particularly if you have a settled job which you enjoy. Complicated travelling arrangements are a constant strain, and the time and temper saved by a shorter, simpler journey could bring rewards – you could gain more time for shopping, cooking, gardening (all money savers!) as well as time for leisure pursuits. One hour per day saves up to seven hours per week – a worthwhile consideration if you plan to use the time saved.

The telephone may come into this category of needs for a number of reasons – business, living alone, elderly parents living some distance away, or living in a remote area. There are other needs in the furnishing and maintenance of the home, and these are considered fully in later chapters.

One expense which many people overlook until it is too late is insurance. This I would rate as a definite need, although it hurts 'to pay for nothing'. You should insure your property and household effects to their full value – any good insurance company will advise you on this. Some people prefer to accept the risk on jewellery, furs and expensive equipment, rather than pay high premiums. After all, you could survive without them, but you would be in a sorry state if you lost your home and its contents for the sake of a few pounds a year.

A daily newspaper, radio and television set will come high on most priority lists. The extra pleasure offered by colour television must be set against the extra cost, although with the escalating price of travel, baby-sitting fees, meals out, and seats at the cinema or theatre it could be considered as a relatively cheap form of family entertainment. Here we enter the realm of choice.

Wants

It has been said that 'yesterday's wants are today's needs'. Wants are things you *can* do without, and this is the area of real choice.

In our present society, we are conditioned to want things. Lift a magazine, switch on television or radio, and you will find someone telling you how to gain the envy of your friends (do you *want* to be envied by them?) in a beautiful complexion, a sexy girl friend or a prize at a dog show – all obtainable by the use of their particular product. Most people will deny that they are influenced by advertising, but it simply is not true. We are all influenced by it, and the influence is not always bad. It can give information and help you make choices, but it does also sow the seeds of desire.

In order to determine your particular needs and wants, write down everything you bought last week. Now tick all the things which you really – honestly – *needed*, and simply could not have done without. The result may surprise you. Then count the cost of the remainder: your wants. That may surprise you even more. If you have to save money, you must make choices from those wants. There is no need to eliminate all wants, but only you can decide which things are most important to you. Use this strategy for all your spending, large and small items alike.

Making choices

Hundreds of niggling economies get tiresome – don't bore yourself and others with them, instead keep a notebook and see how much you are saving and whether some of your efforts are just not worth while. Avoid cutting out all the little things that keep life worth living. The savings are probably not enough to justify the resultant misery. The little things should be cut down though – if chocolate biscuits are kept as a special treat, then there is also the enduring benefit to teeth and waistline!

In some ways, the swingeing economies are less painful; for example the move to a smaller house, which may yield a bigger or better garden. If you are fortunate enough to live near good public transport, consider getting rid of a car. It is cheaper to hire one for holidays and to take taxis in emergencies. Don't bemoan your sacrifices – think positive and look at what can be done with the money saved.

Elderly people who decide reluctantly to part with their car may miss it badly for a number of reasons. They will not, however, miss the large bills for road tax, insurance, servicing, repairs and petrol, and the money saved may go a long way towards paying for the fuel for an efficient and trouble-free central heating system which could be of far more value to them. A young couple may decide to scrap central heating in favour of a car – again the choice is personal. Pay no heed to what everyone else does, or has, or is; it really doesn't matter. What does matter is that your life style is arranged to suit you and your family.

Don't fret about impressing people with expensive food and drink. Serve what you can afford, but do it well. Take a genuine interest in cooking and use fewer convenience foods. Most guests are satisfied and delighted with a bowl of really good home-made soup with hot rolls and perhaps some cheese or fruit. If you serve alcohol, have a go at home-made beer or wine, but do not be offended if it is politely refused! Most people will settle for a cup of tea and good conversation.

Pocket money

However little you can afford, some regular allowance should be made to children, and it is not unreasonable to expect that certain responsibilities be accepted in return. Both allowance and responsibility may increase as the child gets older. You may be amazed at the financial acumen of a ten year old! Whatever the sum, stick to it; there should be no begging for extra money for sweets or the cinema. After all, no benevolent providence furnishes *you* with extras; the budget must be planned to take account of likely extras. As a child gains experience in managing money, you will be saved the constant requests for odd sums which eat into your own budget. Remember, example is important and borrowing should not be encouraged. If you do allow your child to borrow on next week's income, see that the money is repaid. It may seem hard on a twelve year old, for a matter of a few pence, but remember some day he will be a twenty two year old and it may be a few hundred pounds; the principle remains the same.

Hedges against inflation

When prices rise quickly and steeply, any consumer durable bought sooner rather than later will save you money. It must, however, be something which you need, and had intended to buy in the foreseeable future. Such a purchase may involve you in hire purchase or credit (see pp. 16–17) but even this extra cost can be absorbed at the end of the day when inflation persists.

Perhaps the best hedge against inflation is in large-scale investment such as property or precious metal. The most usual choice is a house, since the money can be borrowed for this, and tax relief is obtained on the interest paid while your investment increases in value. There is, of course, no guarantee that property will continue to appreciate in value; but prices are related to the costs of new building, which seem unlikely to fall in any dramatic fashion.

Jumble and junk

Investment in property or precious metals may remain outside the realms of possibility for many of us, but the pursuit of junk and jumble can yield the double-edged pleasure of offering all the fun of a hobby with the expenditure of very little cash. A collection can be formed out of an initial interest in books, dolls, bits and pieces of china or glassware, or any object under the sun. Over the years, collecting can develop into a really absorbing pastime and there is always the dangling carrot of bagging a valuable find.

Investment of time

The investment of time in one of the many and interesting short courses (day or evening) run by most colleges and schools is another proposition worthy of consideration. Hard times make us want to recapture old skills, and much enjoyment and lasting satisfaction can be derived from gaining a new sense of self-sufficiency. It is easy to make enquiries at a convenient school or college or to write to your local education authority. The range of basic, practical courses on offer may surprise you – carpentry, woodworking, car maintenance, electricity, plumbing, plastering, bricklaying, cookery for men and courses on household maintenance specially suited to women, are just a few of the choices. You may even be lucky enough to find crèche facilities so that you can hammer away in perfect peace!

Shopping

Three main points to observe:

Avoid shopping with well-off friends, if you have any.

Avoid browsing and window shopping unless you are carrying no money or means to pay.

Make a list and stick to it – and remember to take it with you.

Household shopping

Time and trouble at the planning stage always save time and money in the shops. Get your store cupboard well-organized, as this will save expensive last-minute forays to the shops.

Allocate a sum for your weekly housekeeping and aim to underspend. Put the money saved into a not-too-accessible place like the Post Office Savings Bank and keep this as a contingency fund to be dipped into for special occasions or for a fair-sized investment such as fruit and sugar for jam-making. Another way of raising a small bank balance is to start your new housekeeping money one day later each week (making the money last for eight days instead of seven). At the end of seven weeks you have a whole week's money 'spare'.

Plan the meals for a week ahead and prepare your shopping list from this, along with your other household needs. Cultivate a critical eye and a steely nerve before you venture into shops. If you have time, shop around, and make use of Consumer Price Surveys where they are displayed in your area. Buy only what is on your list – what you *need*. Loss leaders are of interest only if you need them, and the saving of a few pence will upset the balance of your other items, if you have to spend extra in order to make the so-called saving.

Calculators are often suggested as a means of helping to keep within a budget when supermarket shopping. Fine, if you own a calculator but, if not, your list should do the job for you before you start out. Calculators do not make mistakes, but you can, so be prepared for a recount at the check-out.

Bulk buying

Some people vow it saves a fortune, while others think it wasted effort. This is a highly controversial issue. First of all you must consider – where? It may be possible to make a satisfactory bulk buy arrangement with your local retailer. Most of them will give discount on bulk and cash – if asked! If you have to travel a distance to a town or area you do not normally frequent, remember to count the cost not just in petrol, but also in the A.A.'s reckoning of running cost per mile, which may appal you, but nevertheless remains a fact. If you cannot beg, borrow or otherwise acquire transport, the enterprise is virtually a non-starter.

Storage

Secondly, have you got enough suitable storage space? By suitable, I mean dry, well-ventilated, and free from mice, rats, cats, cockroaches, weevils and other interested parties. You may not have 'incomers' at the moment, but a case of cornflakes in the basement can prove a great attraction, and the word gets round!

Basements provide good storage if the access is easy and if there is no risk of damp or pests. Garages are suspect, as they are often subject to condensation, fumes, and ease of access – to petty thieves in addition to the unwelcome visitors already mentioned. There is also danger from substances like weed-killers, paint removers, anti-freeze and the acids and alkalis which lurk in dark corners in breakable containers.

Attics are another possibility for storage, but be sure that the weight will not be too much for the flooring. A case of canned peaches falling on an unsuspecting head in the middle of the night will hardly be regarded as a bonus, however fond one may have been of canned peaches! On the other hand you could actually insulate the roof with a bulk buy of loo paper, which is also quite light in weight.

Beware of awkward access and struggling to get large packs up rickety ladders or steps. Attics are frequently more access-ible to birds and bats, so take a careful look round before committing your investments to the roof space, and keep a watchful eye on them if you do.

Storage times

There is no economy if you have to throw things away, or eat gargantuan helpings of food before it goes bad. Tins, bottles and jars are a safe bet for storage of up to twelve months, and dry goods like detergents, cereals, and sugar will keep for several months without deterioration. Biscuits and cornflakes will go stale after a few weeks unless you use really airtight containers, so avoid these unless they can be used up quickly. Biscuits could go in the freezer if you have one. Perishables like fruit and vegetables offer some of the biggest savings if you can buy at a market, but long-term storage is out of the question, except for bottling or freezing. Fruit and vegetables might well be considered for group purchase. Sound advice on group purchase is available from the National Consumer Council, 12 Queen Anne's Gate, London SW1; The Scottish Consumer Council, 4 Somerset Place, Glasgow G3; The Welsh Consumer Council, 8 St Andrew's Place, Cardiff CF1 3BE.

Group purchase

A band of like-minded purchasers pooling their resources is a very good idea, but there are complications and it does involve time and trouble for someone – who may be compensated with extra goods. Group purchase should be organized in a business-like fashion or it could be, and often is, the end of flourishing friendships. Someone has to pay the bill at source, and it is much more sensible if everyone contributes a fixed sum towards this bill before the purchase is made, or the unfortunate buyer may find himself well out of pocket if one of the group cannot or will not pay up for his share of the purchase. Again, the cost of transport should be taken into account.

Does bulk buying save?

There are conflicting opinions about this and it depends on many things. Do your sums carefully and look before you leap into spending large amounts of money which may not, in the long run, add up to a saving. Even the enthusiasts of bulk buying warn against one thing – temptation. Large quantities of anything, especially convenient and tasty eatables, lead to extravagant consumption! The fact that the money has been handed over some time ago and forgotten about encourages the idea that you are getting things free. Children *will* help themselves to a bag of crisps from a bulk supply – perhaps you will, too – when they might not go to the trouble and expense of visiting a shop to *buy* a couple of packets. Better stick to things which are basic and dull, like pasta, toothpaste and dog food – no one is likely to run amok with these!

Consider too whether you can stand the monotony of lots of the same. With tinned foods you may have to buy a whole case of one variety so be sure it is popular – don't try something new which three out of four may refuse after the first sample. If you buy large quantities of dry stores like cereals you will probably need bins, tins or similar containers to hold 3-6 kg (7-14 lb). The polythene bags in which these goods are supplied are not entirely satisfactory, as they are fairly easily punctured by man or beast, and difficult to refasten properly, especially if you are in a hurry. Having to provide yourself with special storage containers will mean more expense.

To freezer owners, catering-size tins of fruit represent a reasonable saving, as the remaining contents can be frozen in smaller quantities after the tin has been opened. If you do not have a freezer, the family will have to gorge themselves to use it all up at once, and this is no saving. Naturally, a large family or a party is a different matter.

One last point. To make real savings, you need a fairly substantial capital investment. Ask yourself if £20 tied up in loo paper and tinned tomatoes is the best way to make use of it. Properly invested, the money might earn you more than you are saving, so work it out carefully.

Sales, discounts and second hand

Yes to all three, provided you make planned purchases with all your wits about you. My home is furnished almost entirely with goods which come into one of these three categories and we have seldom had to put up with a really bad buy. Since later chapters refer to sale and second-hand purchases in a variety of areas, only four main points need be mentioned here.

Nothing is a bargain if you do not need it.

You have certain rights and responsibilities as a consumer and you should be aware of them (see chapter 14).

Do not go to your first auction sale alone – go with someone who knows the ropes.

Make use of the small ads in your local paper or newsagent's shop, both for buying and selling. And remember that something you no longer require may be just what someone else is looking for.

Unseen expenses

Large bills for fuel, rates and telephone are all examples of unseen expenses – things for which money is not handed over on receipt of the goods. These bills have an unhappy knack of arriving at the most inconvenient and expensive time of year – after your annual holiday or just before Christmas. The size of the sum demanded is usually outwith your control – the rates may be increased, there may be a spell of exceptionally cold weather, or your teenage daughter may acquire a boy friend at a far distance, resulting in long telephone conversations on your account! The most painless way of coping with these expenses is to set aside regular monthly payments in line with your estimated annual costs. Remember to add a bit on to last year's costs since prices usually rise. As with mortgage repayments, this spreads the cost evenly over the year and makes your budgeting easier, although the payee may benefit from your paying in advance. You will find that most local councils and fuel suppliers will help with an arrangement of this kind. It is a help to have a bank account if you want to do this, as the bank will then take care of the budgeting for you – provided, of course, that you keep the bank supplied with regular funds.

Save it

It seems superfluous to mention fuel saving since it is a topic of national – indeed of international – importance. Excellent booklets and leaflets are available free of charge, covering every aspect including insulation, draught-proofing, double-glazing, lagging, switching off, turning down, and using your common sense. The gas, electricity and solid fuel industries are all active in providing such advice, so do make adequate use of your local centres.

One of the best ways to save fuel would be to persuade shops, offices and schools to reduce their operating temperatures. My experience of all three suggests that most of them are far too hot. This means that when the family return home after sweltering all day, they feel cold in what may be a perfectly *adequate* temperature, so up goes the heating and up go the bills. Certainly, some premises are kept on the chilly side, but this is preferable, as extra clothing can be worn. The warm atmosphere in which many people work is a breeding ground for germs, especially if ventilation is cut down to keep in the heat. Such an atmosphere is also enervating and accounts for much of the unnecessary exhaustion at the end of a working day. Try walking part of the way home in the fresh air instead of taking the bus all the way. You will save three ways – the bus fare, contact with the coughing and sneezing crowds, plus the fact that your inner thermostat will adjust to a cooler and healthier temperature in your own home. The exercise is also free.

Methods of payment
Cash

This is usually the cheapest, and certainly the quickest, way to pay. When a large purchase is made, it is worth asking for a discount if you pay in cash. After all, the firm is not having to wait for the money and, indeed, gains by having it immediately available for reinvestment. Paying by any other method simply puts off the evil day and is unwise if you are working to a tight budget – except in the case of 'spread-the-load-payments' already discussed. It is often saddening but always wise to keep a record of how cash is spent, so that you are never left wondering where it has all gone.

Cheques and credit cards

These do not seem like 'real money', and it is easy to get carried away with the power of a cheque book – until the day the bank statement arrives. Make it a rule never to write a cheque or use a credit card unless you are quite sure you have funds to cover. A cheque book can be used only if you have a bank account, and a bank account is worth having. The 'friendly bank manager' can be a great help in advising on personal budgeting and financial affairs, and a customer with an account regularly in credit can usually rely on help.

Credit

There are many forms of credit, and most of them cost money. If a business has a large number of credit customers, it will also be laying out large sums of money therefore the cost of interest lost and the servicing of the system may be reflected in the cost of the goods. Often the customer will be charged interest on a credit account, so consider carefully before charging large sums. As with cheques, be sure you are going to have the money to pay up when the bill comes in. In days gone by people used to save up for a big item. Today, they buy on credit before an anticipated price rise, then start putting money aside to pay the bill; but money saved earns interest, so it is worth calculating whether it is better to wait and pay cash, especially if a discount can be obtained. Credit accounts are often paid by instalments and if the repayment period is long, the interest charged can add quite a bit to the original cost.

Hire purchase

This is quite different from credit, although on the face of it, the two seem similar. With hire purchase, the goods are literally on hire until you have paid for them, and the company can reclaim them if you default. You also lose any payments you have made, of course. With *credit*, the goods are yours from the start. They cannot be reclaimed and you can sell them if necessary to help pay the bill. Hire purchase companies will usually work out some solution with a hirer who gets into difficulties after one third of the total sum has been paid.

True rate of interest

The amount of interest varies, but it is important to calculate the true rate being paid, which is much higher than may be apparent at first. For example, 10% on £100 over three years is £10 each year, total £30, ignoring any repayments which have been made. This means you are paying interest on the total sum, although your debt is steadily reducing. Hence the true rate of interest is more like 20%. This is an expensive method of payment and should only be used for real needs which you cannot do without. It is very difficult to resist the blandishments of 'have now, pay later' but do realize that it really does cost more in the end, and that you will gain by saving up for your wants instead.

Borrowing

Don't. If you put into practice the advice given in this chapter, it should not be necessary. Borrowing is habit-forming, expensive and dangerous and definitely to be avoided. Unfortunately it is also very tempting to do, but if you fall down on repayment the going can become very rough indeed.

Money lenders and the pawn shop are last desperate resorts and all too often the first step to disaster. Get help and skilled advice from a banker or your local Citizens' Advice Bureau, before it is too late. The ability to manage your finances successfully is an art worth mastering. It asks for self-discipline along with a large measure of applied common sense. You cannot have your cake and eat it, but there are ways of cutting it up so that there are fair shares all round and a little bit left over for another day. Failure to manage this is the difference between solvency and debt or being fed and going hungry, so calculate the size of your slices of cake with care.

chapter 2

FLOOR COVERINGS

Floors have a hard life, a factor which determines to some extent the cost of covering them. There is also a good deal of floor to cover – which means a considerable outlay in financial terms, and a really close examination of the reasons for doing so. Floors are walked on, sat on, spilled and splashed on – how much and how badly depends on the users of the room. Areas of the house which get little use can take cheap floor coverings – they need not also be unattractive. It is unwise to buy top quality coverings if you do not intend to stay in one place for long, unless they are adaptable and can accompany you on the next move. A further important point is the amount of time you can afford to spend in keeping the floor clean. Fortunately, the most expensive floor coverings are not always the most convenient in this respect.

Why cover the floor?

Floors are covered for a variety of reasons: warmth, comfort, appearance, quietness, water resistance and ease of maintenance. Different rooms require different treatment, and some of these reasons become more important than others, depending on the use of the room. Kitchens and bathrooms need water-resistant flooring which is easy to clean; comfort and quietness may be desirable in a bedroom, appearance all-important in a lounge.

The bare floor

Once you have established your own needs in relation to the criteria above, have a good look at the floor, naked and un-adorned, and ask yourself if it needs covering at all. If you detect any creaks or squeaks, locate the offending floorboard and screw it through to the joist in two places. Then silence the edges with talcum powder.

Many older houses have really good floorboards, well worth the effort of sanding, staining and sealing. You can hire a sander quite reasonably and do the job yourself. Modern stains and seals are simple to apply, and the result can look magnificent. If the floorboards bear defacing stains or marks, then it can be very effective simply to paint them the colour of your choice. If you moved into a house with floor covering already in place, investigate what is lurking below it. You can always try staining a small area of floor to get the general effect before you commit yourself to a major undertaking.

Granted, a wooden floor may seem bare and noisy initially, but rugs overcome this problem and they are much cheaper than large areas of carpet. If you feel that a carpet is really necessary, buy the largest square or rectangle the room will take. You will be able to turn this round to distribute wear which means the life of the carpet will be extended considerably.

Non-slip methods
A word of warning – loose laid carpets and rugs can be dangerous, especially where there are children or elderly people, so it is important to prevent slipping and tripping. One method is to nail the carpet down or use special studs, but these do spoil the floor surface. Non-slip underlays can be used. One type available looks like rug canvas and is very effective, but foam plastic sheets are cheaper and just as good. Use the 6 mm ($\frac{1}{4}$ in) thickness and stick it to the underside of the rug with latex-based adhesive, making the foam sheet slightly smaller than the rug or carpet.

Fitted carpets
Fitted carpets are not an economical proposition because of their inflexibility, and because of the amount of carpeting required. You also have to pay for the wastage in fitting. If you look at your room and do a quick calculation of the amount and cost of carpeting underneath furniture and round the edges of the room, you will immediately see the economic advantages of something which can be moved about. Carpet tiles are unquestionably the best buy if you are fixed on the idea of wall-to-wall carpeting. Buy a few extra and use them in rotation, this means you have spares if some get damaged, though stained ones could always be exchanged for those under the sideboard!

Strip carpet
Strip carpet, or 'body' as it is called in the trade, is an

economical buy provided that there is little wastage in matching the pattern. It can be reassembled to fit another room, hall or staircase, or just to spread the wear evenly. Strip carpet may also be used to make the large square or rectangle already suggested. If you flinch at the idea of bare floor round the edges of the carpet, have a surround of cheaper carpet, carpet tiles or felt; lino and vinyl are also good and they come in an extensive range of colour and pattern. It is worth hunting around for off-cuts or oddments of all of these as they can be very cheap indeed and are ideal as surrounds.

Carpet quality
Wool

Traditional pile carpets are made of wool, though this usually contains a small percentage of nylon which adds to already splendid wearing qualities. There are two types of weave, Wilton and Axminster, the latter allowing more flexibility of colour and pattern. The British Carpet Centre have devised a scheme of classification which will help you to select the most suitable quality for your needs.

1 Heavy contract and/or luxury domestic – the most expensive quality.
2 Medium contract and/or heavy domestic – if you can afford it, this gives good value and has a long life.
3 Light contract/general domestic – still expensive, but suitable for the areas in the home which get hard wear – hall, stairs and the most used public room. (If you cannot afford good quality carpets for these areas, it is better to choose an alternative covering, as cheap carpet here is a waste of money.)
4 Medium domestic – suitable for regularly used bedrooms and for public rooms not in general daily use. This would be fine for a lounge which is used only occasionally.
5 Light domestic – again a 'bedroom' quality – good for spare rooms and for any little used area.

Wool carpets are exceptionally hard-wearing, resilient and easy to care for, and dyes are usually fast and reliable. Two colours which may give rise to problems are blue and red, but don't let this put you off, as the manufacturer must accept responsibility for a faulty dye.

Man-made fibres
Those most widely used in modern carpets are nylon, acrylic

fibres and modified rayons, although new techniques are constantly producing others. All of these man-made fibres do wear well, but also have some disadvantages – the electrostatic property which attracts dirt in the first two, and a tendency for the pile to flatten in the last. These disadvantages are being overcome by new finishes and weaves, and there is the compensation that stains can be sponged off easily as the man-mades are less absorbent than wool.

Many of these man-made fibres are used in new types of carpet manufacture (as indeed is wool). They are known as tufted and needlepunched carpets, and have a jute backing frequently bonded on to foam, which gives a pleasantly bouncy surface.

Carpeting which has foam backing is easy to lay and does not as a rule require underlay – an economy worth remembering when you buy. It may not wear quite so well as some woven varieties but as a short-term or light use purchase this type of carpet gives good value. It can also be cut with scissors and needs no finishing or binding.

These manufacturing methods are cheaper but, unfortunately, there is as yet no labelling system as there is for woven wool carpets, so you need good sales advice. Carpets are also made of melded nylon bonded on to a PVC backing. This material is commonly used for carpet tiles which are easy to lay and keep clean, since they can be lifted individually and washed under the tap if necessary.

Jute, sisal and rush

Floor coverings of jute, sisal and rush represent good value for money, as they are hard-wearing and not marred by water splashes. However, they are hard on bare knees and bare feet, and the dirt falls through them so they are not ideal for children's rooms, or for permanent fixing down. They have an attractive appearance and are pleasant and quiet to walk on, with the added advantage of being relatively inexpensive, and, if you are set on a carpet-type floor which will wear well at low cost, these certainly fill the bill.

Colour, pattern and pile

If you want your carpeting to look good for as long as possible, give some thought to the three points above. No doubt you will have a colour scheme in mind, but do remember that pale self-colours are a liability in areas where there are children, animals and other traffic with dirty feet. Small patterns and textures can give an overall plain effect in a much more practical way. Dark self-colours can be almost as bad as pale, since every thread, crumb and bit of fluff will show up to full advantage. Things do get spilled, and there will be marks, stains and burns which you may not be able to remove, so if this is a major buy which is going to have to last a long time, ponder on your family's habits before you choose.

A patterned carpet makes life easier all round, though it may not be what you would prefer purely from the point of view of appearance. Even carpet tiles can be obtained with patterns (though this limits their flexibility somewhat) and you can make up your own pattern using different coloured squares.

Short pile carpets are easiest to keep clean. Shag pile can be obtained in varying qualities, lengths and thicknesses, and looks very luxurious, but it is difficult to keep clean. Imagine trying to clean up a spilled plate of spaghetti or a dropped ashtray or ingrained jellytots! It is not recommended for family eating areas, or, indeed, anywhere that spills may occur.

Hard floor coverings

Linoleum is a tried and trusty old friend; suitable for all areas, not too expensive, and easy to maintain. Lino tiles seem to be the most popular version of this material, principally because they are simple to lay and there is very little wastage. They have to be stuck down; but you can replace worn or badly marked tiles with little difficulty.

Vinyl has properties similar to lino, and is often sold with a cushion backing which gives a more resilient surface to walk on. Colour and patterns are gorgeous and it is very easy to keep clean. It has disadvantages – being plastic it can melt in contact with sufficient heat, and it is very slippery if water or fat is spilled on it.

Rubber and cork are also used as floor coverings, but come into the more expensive categories without having significant advantages to justify the extra outlay.

Wood block floors are expensive, but you can buy these in DIY form, and they will outlast carpet unless the stiletto heel fashion returns – hard wood flooring is very susceptible to indentation.

Laying floor coverings

You must start with a flat floor. An uneven surface will cause uneven wear – and very quickly! Fill any cracks in boards with a home-made paper paste made by tearing paper into small strips and pulping it with boiling water, a little at a time. Then add wallpaper paste and stir until the mixture is very thick. Press this into the gaps with a knife and leave to dry for several days. Plane down uneven joins and if the surface is really past redemption, cover it with hardboard. (In point of fact, hardboard can make a very good floor, sealed or polished.) You can also buy special thick paper to take up unevenness. A level surface is more important for lino and vinyl than for carpet, where the underlay will help to smooth any minor irregularities – but they must be minor.

Underlay

Never be tempted to use either old underlay or – worse still – an old carpet under your new one. Never! The life of your carpet depends more on what you put below it than on what you do on top of it, and your new carpet will promptly start to wear where the one below is worn, since it will not be getting the necessary support. The pile of the carpet below will also exert a 'pull' on the new carpet, and this will cause both movement and wear. Don't economize with cheap underlay if you are investing in top quality carpet. A first-class underlay will also do wonders for a cheaper carpet and extend its life considerably. It is a good idea to lay paper below the felt as this prevents dust and dirt being sucked through the floorboards by the vacuum cleaner.

Vinyl, lino and rubber

Sheet vinyl, lino and rubber can be loose laid, but are much better stuck down, as this prevents the stretching or shrinkage which results in uneven wear. This is a job for an amateur only if skilled, patient and inordinately good-tempered!

Looking after carpeting

Vacuum regularly – how often depends on how much use the room gets and on how many people live in the house. Once a week is usual, oftener as required. Mop up stains and spills right away with something absorbent. Paper, clean dry floor cloths or old towels are all suitable – even not-so-old towels. Towels are easily washed and cleaned and much less expensive than carpet. Don't start sloshing water around until you have soaked up as much of the spill as possible. Once you have done this, sponge with carpet shampoo or a mild liquid detergent. Blot up excess moisture again, and leave to dry. Details of treating individual stains are given in the Stain Removal Guide, chapter 7, where carpets are treated as non-washables.

Carpet shampoos

Carpets, like cats, do not much care for getting wet. It is unwise to overdo shampooing, especially on wool carpets. If your carpet always looks grubby, you may have made a bad choice and there is not much you can do about it, as constant wetting will do nothing to improve it. In the long term you may consider moving it to another less used room and buying something more practical and suited to your needs.

You can have a carpet professionally cleaned, and it is worth the money, provided the carpet is of good quality, as it will come up like new. You never achieve quite the same effect with DIY shampooing – there is an improvement, certainly, but it tends to be short-lived.

Before shampooing, remove as much furniture from the room as possible. Try to do the job on a warm dry day when you can open the windows, and get rid of everyone else in the household, including livestock! Vacuum the carpet thoroughly, then carefully dilute the shampoo according to the instructions which will probably also suggest that you test for dye fastness by treating a small inconspicuous area first. Do so!

Aerosol cleaners are available but they are expensive over large areas. The job can be done by hand, using a rough cloth or a soft brush, but it is much easier with a carpet shampooer. It is possible to hire one, or perhaps you could borrow. Failing this, see if friends or family are willing to share the cost and use of one – it is a good buy, but not an implement that you use very often, so several people sharing one is a good idea, and there is no complicated mechanism to go wrong.

Start at the edges – if the carpet is fitted you will have to do these by hand, as the machine cannot get right up to the skirting board. Otherwise and thereafter, start with the area farthest from the door. Work systematically in squares or strips and *avoid getting the carpet too wet*. This is the most usual mistake. You should wet the pile only, not the backing, otherwise it will take forever to dry, and you may get mildew or shrinkage. When you have finished, allow the carpet to dry completely before vacuuming again (this removes the shampoo and the dirt it has lifted) and replacing the furniture. If furniture has to be left on the damp carpet, place squares of strong polythene under the feet, as any kind of metal fixing or castor could cause rust. Move the furniture a little the next day to allow the carpet which was under the feet to dry.

Worn carpet

Worn carpeting is dangerous, especially on stairs, so do something about it. A stair carpet should have enough extra to allow you to move it up or down, which helps to lengthen its life considerably. Any frayed parts should be cut out and the edges rejoined with self-adhesive binding, or ordinary carpet binding and Copydex, which makes a stronger repair. Try to place the join at the angle of tread and riser where it will be less obvious.

Protect carpets from wear by fitting castors to furniture which is moved a lot. Plastic cups are available to fit under the legs of beds, chairs and tables. Make a point of using a hearthrug in front of the fireplace where much of the use and abuse of carpets occur.

Patching carpets

Unless you are terribly well-organized, it is unlikely that you will have a spare piece of carpet to use for a patch, so you will have to remove a square from under a piece of furniture. If the pattern is very large, you will have more of a problem. Before you give in to despair – or even look around for a suitable patch – stop and survey the situation. There might be a simpler answer. Can you either move the whole carpet round, making a fitted carpet into a loose laid one, or move the furniture, so that the damaged part is no longer in evidence?

A patch is best done when the carpet is still in good condition and there is only a small area of damage. Putting a new piece of carpet in the middle of a well-worn area can look more obvious than wear! You will find it easier to make an accurate patch if you turn back the carpet to cut out the damaged area from underneath. A patch is not particularly difficult to do (see p. 26) but it must be neatly cut and stuck down firmly, so take time to make a good job of it, ensuring that when the patch is in place the pile is lying in the right direction for the rest of the carpet.

Note: Watch out for moth and carpet beetle damage in dark corners and under furniture. Guinea pigs also enjoy a diet of carpet, so beware of allowing such pets into a carpeted area!

To patch a carpet

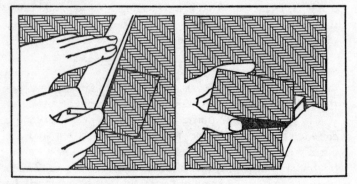

1 Mark a square with chalk round the damaged area, making sure square aligns with weave of carpet. (You can stop edges from fraying by coating latex-based adhesive all round square and rubbing it in.)
2 Cut out square with a sharp knife

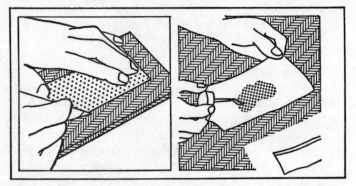

3 Cut out patch from repairing material
4 Coat hessian with latex-based adhesive

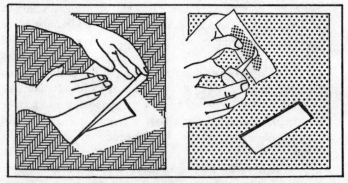

5 Stick hessian over square hole in the carpet
6 Coat patch with adhesive, particularly the edges, and fix in place

Care of hard floors

They need sweeping and washing. Ingrained dirt causes wear. Vinyl, lino, rubber and wood floors can all be sealed to cut down on maintenance but be sure you buy the right kind of seal for the floor and apply it according to instructions. Correct preparation of the floor is all-important. Solvent-based seals can damage vinyl, lino and rubber. Seals need to be renewed as they wear off. Polish is good for lino and wood floors, but it does mean extra effort.

Stains do not, as a rule, present much difficulty on hard floors, since they are unlikely to penetrate. Heat and solvents can damage vinyl, while linoleum can be spoiled and 'dried out' by too much washing and the use of harsh detergents. Water can seep between lino tiles and loosen the backing, so a good initial polish or seal followed up by a regular damp mopping is the most successful method of maintenance.

Patching

If damage occurs, the patching method is similar to that used for carpet, but in this case the patch may be cut in one with the removal of the damaged part. Place the repairing piece over the hole, matching the pattern if any. Mark out a suitably sized square or oblong. *Lightly* tack or stick the patch to the floor, and using a sharp knife, cut round the marked square, right through the flooring also. Remove both pieces and, after any necessary tidying of sub-floor, stick the new piece firmly in position.

Sales and seconds

Never go shopping for floor coverings without a scale plan of your room. Sale carpets can be great bargains, especially samples and 'end of ranges'. Make enquiries about 'seconds' – flaws in the pattern are the most usual reason for this label, and they are often very minor. This means you can get a top quality carpet substantially reduced in price. Sometimes there is a hole, a burn, or a stain – in this case the price may be even further reduced, and if it so happens that your furniture would cover it or the shape of your room would allow it to be cut out, you are on to a good thing. Fire and water damaged stock should be viewed with great care and some suspicion. Water marks may not come out and smoke soiling is difficult to remove.

Beware of street markets and 'one-night-stand' carpet sales. Goods *can* be genuine and there are bargains, but you need all your wits about you. You do have rights as a buyer but you may find it difficult to secure them if the goods turn out to be faulty. It usually takes some time for carpet faults to become evident – other than those mentioned above – meantime, the seller has moved on to new pastures and you may not even hold a receipt.

Second hand

Auction sales and private sellers are worth considering as a means of securing nearly new floor coverings at very reasonable prices. People can make expensive mistakes in their choice of carpet and, if they are lucky enough to be able to try again, *you* may cash in. Fortunately, tastes in carpet design vary enough to make someone else's 'poison' your 'meat'. Remember that strip carpeting can be split up, which gives it flexibility of use – again you need your measurements and a measuring tape handy. Inspect carpets for moth damage – small holes can be made good with matching wool. You can manage with a short darning needle but a proper carpet needle or curved upholstery one is better. Use the wool double and loop it into the jute backing. Leave long ends and trim off evenly once the hole is filled.

Bargains in lino are worth looking for – pieces from large houses, even if worn in places, can often yield enough for a bathroom, hall or kitchen at a very low price indeed. Even unpromising lino, provided it is not actually cracked, can be improved beyond all recognition by a good coat of wax polish. You can also paint with reasonable success, but use proper lino paint.

Last point

Make your own! Not necessarily a whole carpet, though it has often been done. Rug making is an interesting hobby, and though the materials seem expensive, the result far surpasses anything you could buy for the same money. The finished article adds a real touch of luxury and individuality to any room, and it will wear forever.

chapter 3

FURNITURE

Homes are furnished more by fashion and tradition than by a critical assessment of what is actually required. Hard-up youngsters are often much more practical and successful when it comes to determining furnishing needs than those who are better off – they have to be!

Buying furniture

When you go shopping, there are a number of important general points to bear in mind when making your selection. The first one, apart from the amount of money you can afford to spend, is the size of the room you are furnishing. In a large showroom, a piece of furniture looks much smaller than it does in the average home, so take a scale plan of your room with you. Remember that large items may have to be negotiated round corners, up stairs and through awkward doorways. It is wise to size up these hazards before making a final decision on your purchase.

Furniture may be constructed from solid wood which is expensive and not widely used in the popular price range. Nevertheless, it is a sound investment if you intend to keep your furniture for a lifetime, as it will take almost any amount of hard usage. Pieces will usually be labelled, but you can recognize it by seeing the 'end grain' at the edges of shelves and tables. The most usual material for modern furniture construction is veneered chipboard, blockboard or plywood. Quality varies a lot, so look for well-matched veneers, neat joins and edges properly finished with solid wood strips. A veneer strip along the edge is much less durable.

Look at the back of furniture and underneath it. Poor workmanship will be evident in rough edges, bad joints, blobs of glue and the use of nails instead of screws. Examine the finish of edges and corners, and the inside of drawers and cupboards. Drawers should run smoothly and doors open and close easily on strong hinges; long doors need more than two hinges. Catches should be positive and handles easy to grasp and use, with no sharp edges. Notice whether the furniture is well-balanced – open both wardrobe doors and all the drawers in a chest to see whether there is a tendency for these pieces to tip forward. A wardrobe should be long enough for full length dresses and wide enough for coathangers plus garments.

Dining chairs should be sturdy and strongly made. Sit on them to see whether the back rest is comfortable and try rocking on the back legs. We all know this is bad practice, but you can be sure it will be done, so it is worth checking for visible or audible protest!

Up until quite recently, fashion dictated that furniture came in suites, and shops could make you buy two wardrobes and a dressing table as a set, or a settee and two matching armchairs, regardless of your wants, needs, size of room or bank balance. All is now changed, ranges of matching furniture are widely available and you may purchase the pieces you need as you can afford them, adding others later. This has the great advantage that you can invest in good quality furniture – some ranges have been on the market for well over twenty years. And furnishing on this basis allows you to add items from other ranges and periods with no restrictions other than your own taste.

Buy what you need, and what you like. Rooms are for living in, not for displaying the craftsman's art. Comfort and convenience are prime considerations – think about how the room will be used as this settles most of the questions about choice of furniture and furnishings. There is no point in having a sideboard if you have nothing to put in it, or a piano if no one plays. Don't clutter up the place with occasional tables and chairs if they will not be used. They make extra work for you and the room will look more spacious without them.

What do you need?

Basically you need things to sit on, eat off, work on, sleep on and store things in. These needs will vary according to circumstances and the aim today is to make your furnishing system as flexible as possible so that fullest use can be made of all the rooms in the home.

Types of seating

One could sit on the floor – many people like to – but this preference is unlikely to be shared by all your friends and family, so the required number of chairs must be established. It should be possible for everyone in the household to have a reasonably comfortable seat. Upholstered furniture today is much more casual than the traditional 'three-piece suite' which takes up a great deal of space in a small room and is an expensive item to buy. Single chairs which can be grouped in different ways make a much more adaptable system.

Upholstered furniture

You can see only the covering, which is no advantage if you are looking for strong construction which will stand up to the rigours of family living. In the past, this type of furniture had a wooden frame, metal coil springs and horsehair and flock padding. Modern techniques use rubber webbing and horizontal, narrow springs, with latex or polyether foam for comfort, and the frame of the chair may be a plastic shell. Do not economize on chairs which will be in daily use. Cheap ones will look shabby and become damaged in no time. If you cannot afford to buy good new chairs, look for good second-hand. Stretch nylon covers will renew their appearance and you can buy new seat cushions if these are worn.

Price is the main guide to quality, but you can save money in the long run by a thoughtful choice at the outset. Wooden arms will not wear out or become soiled like upholstered ones, and there is less temptation to perch on wood – a practice ruinous to any armchair. Naturally, you will select a chair which is comfortable, but remember comfort means different things to different people so consider the sitters when you buy. Elderly people prefer an upright chair with a fairly high seat, for example, while knitters like chairs without arms.

Look for firm construction and well-fitted covers with neatly finished edges. Reversible cushions help to distribute wear, and even better are chairs with covers which can be removed for washing or dry cleaning. Covers should be practical in colouring, hard-wearing and easy to clean. Some manufacturers now have excellent labelling.

Coverings and care

Leather	hard-wearing, but expensive. Clean with leather soap.
Vinyl	usually backed with fabric – this is the best kind. Waterproof and not easily stained except by biro ink and some hair oils and creams. Clean with soap and water. Never use solvents.

Brocade and Damask	very elegant, but neither hard-wearing nor easy to keep clean.
Tweed	reasonably priced and also reasonably hard-wearing.
Moquette	a traditional upholstery fabric with a looped or cut pile. Expensive and usually hard-wearing. Avoid it if you are owned by a cat who will love pulling out the loops with its claws.
Velvet	modern upholstery velvet is usually a man-made fibre, Dralon. It wears well but can show marks and is not very practical in daily use.

The last three materials can be cleaned quite well by sponging with a suitable upholstery shampoo, but be careful not to soak them. Cleaning must be done before the fabric becomes too dirty, or the result may be watermarked and patchy. Always test on an inconspicuous part as the colour may be affected and you don't want this to happen in the most obvious place. A spirit cleaner like Beaucaire or Thawpit can be used on most fabrics. Apply lightly with a clean rag. Keep changing the rag as it becomes soiled, otherwise you will simply spread the dirt around. Pay particular attention to head and arm rests, which become greasy. Run the vacuum cleaner over upholstery regularly. If you do not have a suitable attachment, brush the upholstery gently. Remember that fabric furniture collects as much dust as wooden-surfaced furniture. The snag is that it doesn't show so the tendency is to forget about it, but every time a weighty adult sits on a chair, all the dust is ground into the upholstery, causing both soiling and wear.

Extra seating

If you need extra seating, cast an eye over folding garden and picnic furniture, the cheaper kinds of cane chair, floor cushions and inflatable furniture. They can also be used in bedrooms, and are easily portable for an unexpected flurry of guests.

Beds

A bed is a priority: you spend about one third of your life in it. Beds come in assorted shapes, sizes and qualities. So do the people who sleep in them, therefore making a choice is not always easy. As with upholstered furniture, the main visible influence is the cover which is about the last thing to consider, though people have been known to choose on this alone!

Size

Bedrooms get smaller while beds get bigger and the country must be full of quart-size beds in pint-size bedrooms. Builders of houses and beds ought to get together. Before shopping for a new bed, especially if you plan to have a larger one, do a measuring exercise or draw a scale plan of the bedroom. A bed 15 cm (6 in) wider than your present model will carve ·28 sq m (3 sq ft) off your bedroom floor space, which you can probably ill afford. You must consider whether your present bed linen will be adequate. If not, you will be risking laying up further expense.

Metric beds are 150 cm/4′11″ (double) or 100 cm/3′3⅜″ (single) and will take up considerably more room than any previous bed. The 'old' regular sizes are still on sale as well as the smaller 75 cm (2′6″) which is suitable for a child or as an occasional bed for the spare room. This size is also worth considering if you want to have two beds in a small room.

Twin beds take up more space than a double bed, and cost almost twice as much to buy. Linen requires to be duplicated and there is twice as much washing to be done, so they are anything but economical! This is a choice for the individuals concerned but the the expense of such a choice should be appreciated. For chilly mortals, two electric blankets would be needed, and even two hot water bottles cost more than one!

Special children's beds can be bought, but as children grow so quickly they may as well graduate from cot to a normal single bed. Bunk beds save space, but are best used with sleeping bags or continental quilts, as they are so difficult to make, especially if placed, as is most usual, in a corner.

Quality

Once again price is the best guide to quality along with a reliable brand name, but it does pay to shop around. The difference in price for the same model is often very marked. Usually a manufacturer who makes beds in a wide price range gives good value at all levels. Comfort is more important than an attractive cover (which no one will see) so do test for comfort by lying on the bed in the shop. It is expected that you will and a cover is provided to protect the bed from your shoes.

There are two main types of mattress filling on the market – spring interior and foam – and both are obtainable in various qualities. The more expensive spring interiors will have a greater number of springs, individually pocketed, at the top end of the price range. The padding may consist of wool, cotton, foam or man-made fibres.

Foam mattresses may be either latex rubber or polyether foam, sometimes both in variously sandwiched layers. In either type of bed the degree of firmness may vary considerably, and this too, is a matter for individual choice. Do not assume that a hard bed will last longer!

When beds are for regular nightly use, buy the best you can afford. It is false economy – martyrdom even – to attempt to sacrifice decent comfort in bed. For seldom used spare room beds, a cheaper model is quite suitable and comfortable, as it will have much less wear and tear. With divans, the mattress and base are designed as a unit, so buy both at the same time. Look for the British Standards Institution Kitemark (pp. 156–7) which is an indication of an established standard of requirements and is a useful guide especially when buying a cheaper bed. More expensive beds will exceed the BSI standard. Latex or foam is a wise buy for people who are allergic to fluff and dust, and also a good buy for children's beds as accidents and fairly predictable spills will not be absorbed to any significant depth.

Extra beds

If you have no spare bedroom but expect occasional overnight guests, there is a wide variety of sofa-beds, put-u-ups and folding beds available. All of these are fairly expensive and a cheap, useful and space-saving alternative is an air-bed used in conjunction with a sleeping bag. They can also be used for camping, the beach and the garden during the summer. Folding garden beds are a possibility too but are more suitable for children, as they are on the narrow side for a good night's rest, and have a hard metal edge. Adults need more room to turn over or curl up during sleep when the posture is quite different from that adopted for an hour or two's sunbathing. The air bed is the more comfortable of the two, and you can adjust the air content until it suits the user.

Eating, working and storage
Tables

A dining table should seat the family and, ideally, be expandable enough to take a few extra. The shape of a table is important – a round one accommodates more people than a square or oblong of the same area, but it takes up more room. If you wish to use more than four oblong place mats a round table begins to look peculiar, and cloths can be a problem, if you use them. A large table in a small room is an absolute pest – half your life is spent dodging round it, the other half nursing bruises which result from unavoidable collision with the corners. So choose a table which folds up or down for a small room which is used for family living as well as dining. Check that the folding mechanism is simple to use and unlikely to amputate fingers, and also that gate legs do not shut uncontrollably whenever someone knocks against them. It should also be possible to seat everyone comfortably with human legs easily avoiding table legs.

A table should be firm, sturdy and strongly made. It is likely to be used for all sorts of unlikely purposes, so, unless it is to be kept solely as a dining table, give ample thought to the use and abuse it will receive at the hands of your family. Homework, model making, cutting out, table tennis, jigsaw puzzles and pasting wallpaper are but a few uses in addition to serving as a parking space for the sewing machine, record player, typewriter and, in extremes, minor engineering projects on the vacuum cleaner! Solid wood is expensive, but can be sanded and repolished, which is not always possible with veneer.

The same points apply to the kitchen table, if you are lucky enough to have room for one. This is quite the most useful work space in the house, mainly because you can sit down at it. Perching on a high stool in front of a work top or breakfast bar is not the same at all, and there are many jobs for which a table is a more comfortable working height than the normal kitchen unit. A kitchen table can also relieve the dining table of much abuse.

Storage

Generous storage can be managed without breaking the bank, thanks to the wide range of versatile units now available. Knock-down furniture (which always seems a contradiction in terms since you actually have to knock it up!) saves money both in transport costs and in tax, and is relatively easily assembled by the average handy person. Whitewood furniture is excellent value and can be painted to suit your fancy.

China and cutlery are most handily kept by the dining area, traditionally in a sideboard which usually matched the table and chairs. There is no law about this, and cupboards or chests of drawers may prove more useful. Clothes-hanging space is at a premium in most homes and should be reasonably dust- and moth-proof. Built-in cupboards can often be arranged in alcoves and corners. But do not spend a lot of money on them if you are likely to move house, as, strictly speaking, built-in furniture is a fixture which you cannot take with you. At a pinch, a high wide shelf with a curtain screen will serve as a wardrobe, but it would be wise to buy large plastic bags to cover your more expensive clothes.

Sturdy wooden packing cases can be padded and covered with fabric to give inexpensive but effective storage and seating. And dressed or veneered planks of wood stacked on painted or varnished bricks make useful bookshelves. Don't overlook the potential of strong cardboard boxes, especially for children's books, toys and games, or, turned upside down and covered with wallpaper or Fablon, they make useful bedside tables as there is not likely to be much weight on them. Little used articles can be stored in them, wrapped in polythene bags for extra protection if necessary.

The kitchen is one of the main storage areas in the home, and it can be streamlined, modern and attractive without spending a fortune on expensive units. Admittedly, the DIY expert has a great advantage here, but initial attention to the planning of unit runs and careful shopping around can save a surprising amount of money. Plumbing and electrical alterations are expensive and to be avoided if a reasonable compromise is possible. Adequate and suitable storage space in the kitchen is essential, particularly for food. Many local authorities have a bye-law which ensures that every house must be provided with a suitably ventilated cupboard for this purpose. A reminder that built-in kitchen units are also considered as fixtures – so avoid spending lavishly if you are a bird of passage, unless the house is your own and you look on the expenditure as an investment towards a better sale value.

Children's rooms
Money can be wasted in decorating nurseries in nursery style. Babies will not be aware of it, and older children like to change things to suit themselves. Decorate a room simply, with hard-wearing washable surfaces. Provide a wall area which can be scribbled on and wiped clean then the other walls in the house may escape attention. Storage space is required for clothes and toys and this can be arranged quite inexpensively. A work surface, table or desk will be needed – a wide shelf would do –

with pegboard or pin board above so that posters and pictures can be mounted without marking the walls. At least one chair is needed, and the bed should be covered with something durable and easily washable, as it will be used both as a seat and a play area. A plaid rug or blanket is as good as anything: it is warm to sit on, easily washed and needs no ironing. The floor can be covered with vinyl or lino with non-slip surface and a rug. Carpet is warmer but do not buy a new one – this is a good room to use up oddments.

Furniture care

Save money by choosing surfaces which are hard-wearing and easy to care for, as they will continue to look good for many years. When buying always ask for care instructions. You may not get them, but if we all keep asking, the message should get through. Many manufacturers do provide information and advice, and since you can do a lot of damage – quite unintentionally – by using the wrong sort of cleaner or polish, it is always worth looking for reliable guidelines.

Wood finishes

There are a number of protective finishes for wood and they all require different treatment.

Wax-polished furniture should be treated with a standard wax furniture polish, available as both a paste and a cream. You can make your own from this recipe:

Multi-purpose polish
Melt a 30 gm (1¼ oz) candle with 75 gm (3 oz) beeswax (obtainable from hardware store or chemist). Add ½ litre (1 pint) turpentine. Stir this until it cools and thickens slightly. Now dissolve 1 tablespoon mild detergent (like Dreft) in ½ litre (1 pint) hot water. Add this to the turps mixture and place the pan in cold water. Stir till thick and creamy. Bottle and label. You can use this on all surfaces where a wax polish is suitable – including shoes!

Oiled wood should not be polished. Dust regularly and occasionally rub lightly with teak oil or cream. Lavish use of oil or cream will result in a sticky goo, so be careful in the application. Don't expect, or try for, a shine. This furniture is meant to have a matt finish.

French polish has a very high gloss, and requires only dusting and occasional attention with furniture cream.

Mass-produced wood finishes benefit from occasional polishing, but if the furniture has a permanent seal finish you will be wasting time, energy and polish.

Painted furniture should be washed with soap or detergent and water. A very mild abrasive like Jif or Chemico can be used on stubborn marks. Restore the finish with furniture polish.

Plastic can be very difficult to wash clean. Ordinary bar soap gives as good a result as anything, and seems to help cut down the static which attracts dirt. Furniture polish can be used.

Simple disaster procedures

Spills and splashes mop up AT ONCE, before they have time to do damage.

Heat marks try Brasso, it is often effective. You will need to repolish afterwards. Heat marks do fade in time, unless they are very bad.

Cigarette burns use very fine steel wool, followed by linseed oil.

Scratches use brown shoe polish. You can buy a special scratch cover polish, but the shoe polish will probably be in the house anyway. Iodine can be applied with a fine paint brush.

Dents can occur for a number of reasons, often unexplained! They can sometimes be steamed out with an iron and damp cloth, though there is a risk of causing a burn mark. Or you could try keeping a damp cloth in contact with the dent for several hours.

Really bad dents and scratches can be removed by sanding and repolishing, but some wooden furniture has a very thin veneer and this would be better tackled professionally – and probably expensively. There are two other possibilities if you cannot afford this, or feel the article is not worth the expense: resurface with Fablon or with plastic laminate in a simulated wood finish.

Wine and spirit marks often impossible to remove if left for any length of time. If the marks are light, rub with cigarette ash, then polish up.

To remove a build-up of polish on furniture wipe over with a cloth wrung out of vinegar and water – 1 or 2 tablespoons vinegar to $\frac{1}{2}$ litre (1 pint) water. Cold tea can be used very successfully to clean varnished wood.

Note: aerosol products are convenient BUT – expensive, extravagant, unnecessary, pollutant and to be avoided!

Sales and discount buying

As with most other household goods, sharp eyes at sale time can yield considerable savings, especially in furniture with minor damage – in most homes it will soon acquire a few scratches and dents, so one to start with will not matter too much. Showroom pieces with slight damage or minor soiling of upholstery are often sold off at very attractive prices – just be sure you need them! Big discounts are sometimes offered at warehouses and cash and carry establishments. This furniture is usually from the less expensive ranges, and though you can get bargains, it is often worth noting the prices in furniture shops. There may be surprisingly little difference, and the shop will also deliver the furniture as a rule. Cash and carry usually means what it says – this could mean extra cost for you in transporting your prize home.

Smaller items of furniture, furniture in kit form, bookcases, trolleys and occasional tables are regularly advertised direct from the manufacturer with obvious savings on retail prices. This method of buying has the slight disadvantage that you cannot inspect what you are getting until it arrives, and then it may prove disappointing in the cold light of day. But most of these offers carry a money-back guarantee.

Mail order is an attractive way of buying furniture for those who live in remote areas. It is an expensive way to buy, but it may well prove less expensive than a journey to the nearest town which has suitable shops and consequent high delivery charges.

Buying second hand

Any home can be beautifully – and completely – furnished for a fraction of the cost of new furniture. There are a number of ways of buying second hand. You can visit a saleroom or attend local auction sales. Newspaper 'For Sale' columns and the fascinating displays of postcard advertisements in shop windows are often the source of real bargains.

Auctions

It is usually possible for you to view the goods before an auction sale, so that you have a chance to examine them thoroughly. This is important, since it is a case of *caveat emptor* – let the buyer beware – and it is up to you to satisfy yourself about the state of the article you mean to buy. Look for signs of damage and decide whether you can repair it easily and cheaply. Look out also for the small, even holes which spell woodworm. It is risky to take this into your home, although it can be successfully treated. If you decide that something *is* for you, make up your mind quite firmly what you are prepared to pay. Allow up to 50p over a round figure – other people tend to stop bidding *on* this – and another 10 or 15p which will often secure the article. You are responsible for paying immediately, and also for the removal of your purchase as a rule.

Enquire about delivery before you buy a Victorian mahogany wardrobe! Consider the potential 'break down' value of such items, even if you don't want a wardrobe – the wood is often beautifully grained and could be made into a coffee table, bookcases or a bedhead. (Classes in woodwork are a first-rate investment.)

If you cannot be present at the actual sale, ask a porter if he will bid for you telling him your limit. The alarming stories one hears of people being saddled with wildly expensive antiques because they waved a handerkchief at the wrong moment are largely untrue. An auctioneer recognizes a serious bid! Go with a friend who knows the ropes, or go alone to watch the proceedings before you get involved in buying.

Restoring looks

Second hand buying has great potential, but you must learn to see beyond unpromising first appearances. Don't be too easily put off. Everyone will go for the things which are in top condition, and they may pay sweetly for them, too. Consider what a coat of paint or varnish could do, some new hinges or handles, a fresh cover, or even a good wash!

Hideous Victorian monstrosities to which you would not give house room can be transformed into beautiful pieces of furniture when stripped of some of their ornate embellishments, so look around junk shops, second hand shops and family attics. There is something very therapeutic about restoring old furniture and this is one of the more enjoyable economies.

Quick tip: to remove old varnish or paint from carved or awkward pieces, brush with paint remover, leave to soak, then rinse off quickly with the hose. Do not allow wood to stay wet, or it may warp. Naturally this demands time and effort but you do save money.

chapter 4

EQUIPMENT

Expensive electrical equipment may justify the expenditure when it also appreciably improves the quality of life which cannot ever be measured in purely financial terms. Costly equipment can qualify as a need in a household where two people are gainfully employed. Time for housework will be limited, to say nothing of energy, and the savings in time and temper may well justify the expense. But think carefully and choose wisely before committing yourself to a big outlay or hire purchase repayment on something which may in the end prove disappointing. Running costs (see pp. 143–4) and servicing should be included in your sums, and the equipment must be suitable for your own particular requirements. Someone else's 'best buy' could be a financial disaster for you. Too many people are seduced into buying expensive equipment because it is owned and liked by friends who may have more money and who may genuinely require the article (they *may* also be trying to justify their own outlay). Advertising also plays a large part in this field. Remember that no washing machine yet invented is able to present you with the pile of neatly ironed spotless articles shown in the advertisement. Some effort on your part is necessary. The same goes for freezers full of delectable dishes – *you* have to buy and prepare the food.

Cookers
You may cook on a brand new, a second-hand or reconditioned cooker but you will want to cook somehow – or at least be able to heat food. Choosing a cooker today can be a daunting experience, as so many types are available. Fuels used are electricity, gas – town, natural or bottled – solid fuel and oil. Most people have their own preference, and apart from the fact that solid fuel cookers frequently heat the water supply there is not much to choose between them for running costs.

Solid fuel cookers
The installation of a solid fuel cooker is a fairly major and

expensive undertaking and, once installed, it takes up a good deal of space. It keeps the kitchen pleasantly warm in winter, but perhaps too hot in summer. A certain amount of dust and dirt is unavoidable, and the heat is difficult to control. You cannot have a grill on a solid fuel cooker.

Gas and electric cookers

These are available in various sizes and with a number of refinements, all of which cost money. Too small a cooker will drive you mad; a larger one is not very much more expensive and well worth it if you have enough space. You can make more use of the larger oven when it is on, by filling it to capacity, and there are other features, discussed below, which can prove to be economical.

Time control ovens

It would be interesting to know how many people possess time controls on cookers and never use them! Ask yourself if you will use this gadget. What for? If you are out at work all day, and you have the energy to organize everything the night before, you can return to a piping hot meal *provided:* the controls are properly set, the cooker is switched on, there has not been a power cut or failure, you have not been extensively delayed. Time controls can be very useful but only to the well-organized. It does cost extra to have this gadget on a cooker, but you may find it difficult nowadays to buy a new cooker without one. This may be a case of supply, demand and crossed wires!

Variable size hotplates

Electric cookers are more versatile if they have hotplates of different sizes. A pan should cover the entire heated surface, if it does not, the unused area simply serves to heat the kitchen. People who often use small pans should look for a cooker with at least one small plate, or the 'dual' kind which will heat the centre part of the plate only. Gas cookers often have a burner with fewer jets for the same purpose, or for slow cooking. The gas flame should never come up the sides of the pan.

Double grills

The grill is an expensive way of cooking, even though it is quick. 'Dry' frying in a pan on the hotplate is cheaper. In the larger cookers a double grill is often available and this can cut the cost of cooking small quantities, since only half the element is used. Unfortunately, it is usually the same half every time, which means you cannot spread the wear. This is an extra worth having.

Fan ovens
The theory of a fan oven is that it will cook things more quickly and evenly. The heat of the oven is the same throughout, which is useful for batch baking large quantities; not so useful for a complete meal where the various dishes need different temperatures and you want to space them accordingly. Fan ovens are sometimes noisy and there is no way of testing this in the store. This is a point to remember with most motor-driven electric equipment – fridges, freezers, washing machines, driers and vacuum cleaners. Noise affects people in different ways, and some people can lose sleep due to the vibration and hum of a freezer downstairs or in the garage. It is a pity that there is no way of knowing how noisy the motor is until it is firmly established in your home. Do all you can to find out before you buy. Ask in the shop, consult friends and any relevant literature – such as *Which?* – that you can lay hands on.

Double ovens
In many newer models, the grill chamber doubles as an extra oven. This is very useful and economical for small amounts of food, meals for one or two, warming plates and keeping food hot. It is well worth considering in relation to the extra cost.

Self-cleaning ovens
Some grill and oven linings have a special dull surface which does not require cleaning, though it still *looks* as if it did, and you will spoil the surface if you do try to clean it.

The real self-clean ovens use vast amounts of electricity and are not in the economy class at all. Due care in cooking by using covered roasters and casseroles, and a little regular work with Brillo and a damp cloth are much cheaper and just as effective. (See also p. 132.)

Spit-roasters
These are for the very gadget-conscious and for the people who enjoy cleaning ovens. Do you? A spit-roaster takes a little time and dexterity to assemble and the oven takes much time and elbow grease to clean. The food is very tasty, and you might

consider such an item worth the extra money. Spit-roasting incidentally, is not for the cheaper cuts of meat, so those on the track of real economy could well pass this gadget by.

Refrigerators

Most people would class a refrigerator as a need. It does save money by keeping food fresh and allowing you to shop at times in the week when prices are lower and shops less busy. Running costs are almost negligible and they can be kept to a minimum by regular defrosting – automatic defrosting is available on many models. In the popular price range refrigerators do not vary widely in price and are not usually supplied with much in the way of extras. Buy a size to suit the available space, your purse and your family needs. Allow $1\frac{1}{2}$ cubic feet per person – minimum 4 cubic feet. Check that there is room for tall bottles and also that there is a variety of shelf adjustment. It should be possible to store frozen food, but a refrigerator is not suitable for *freezing* food. You can live without a refrigerator, especially if you have a really cold larder, but there are wiser economies to be made.

Vacuum cleaners

Even if you have no carpets a suction cleaner is worth having, and a cylinder model is the sensible choice as it is supplied with nozzles for cleaning practically everything. It removes dust quickly and efficiently, where a brush would spread it around, and adds to the life of upholstery and furnishings by removing dust and dirt which are the cause of much wear and tear.

The upright cleaner often beats carpets in addition to sucking up dirt, and a good cleaner will certainly add to the life of your carpets and rugs by removing grit and soiling from deep within the pile. An upright is not the most convenient cleaner for stairs – the cylinder-type proves more adaptable.

When buying, consider the variety of attachments in relation to the cleaning you have to do, and also dustbags and their cost. Some models may be used with, or without, bags.

Like the refrigerator, the vacuum cleaner is not essential for your survival, but it does save money by prolonging the life of carpets, upholstery and furnishings, and it does save time. The running cost is very low. Look for a good brand name.

Washing machines

It is a fact of life that clothes have to be washed. The method can vary. You can use the services of a laundry, but the cost is likely to be so astronomical that the idea is hardly worth consideration. Launderettes frequently provide the answer, although they have limitations, do not necessarily give the best possible result, and are not always readily available. Hand washing is very hard work, although there are ways of reducing the labour (discussed in chapter 6) and it is certainly the cheapest method. It can take up a considerable amount of time. A spin drier would come higher than a washing machine on my list of priorities, since drying is usually more of a problem than washing.

There are three types of washing machine:

Single tub
These consist of a washer, usually with a heater and wringer. They are cheapest to buy, use and maintain, being relatively simple mechanically.

Twin tub
A single tub and spin drier in the same unit. More expensive than a single tub, since you are getting a spin drier – in which you can rinse – as well. Twin tubs have refinements like thermostatic controls which trigger the wash mechanism and automatic rinsing. There is obviously more to go wrong, but putting it right is fairly straightforward. They are quick and quite economical to use.

Automatic
Put in washing, set and forget. That, at least, is the theory! The controls of these machines are more sophisticated and this you have to pay for. Remember to allow for the cost of installation if plumbing is required. They save time, because you are not involved, but the wash process does take longer. The water and powder can be used only once – this means you need fresh hot water and powder for every load of washing.

If things go wrong, it can be expensive to have them put right. Properly used, an automatic could save you money, by washing everything in the most efficient way on the correct programme. Sad to say, few people do use them properly. The biggest advantage is time- and labour-saving – important points for a working family. A washing machine is not a need. You can survive amazingly well without one.

Driers

There is no question of any *choice* between spin and tumble driers, as they serve completely different purposes. The spin drier removes water after washing in the same way as, but more efficiently than, a wringer. The tumble drier takes the place of the clothes line. It is expensive to use – the most efficient way is to fill it only two thirds full. It works by tumbling clothes in a current of hot air. Heating anything is expensive, and there is a certain amount of wear and tear on textiles in the tumbling. This is no kind of money-saver, especially if you have any other means of getting clothes dry. The spin drier, on the other hand, removes a great amount of water and this means that the clothes dry more rapidly. The clothes themselves do not move in the drier, so there is no wear.

If clothes must be dried indoors and electricity has to be used, the tumble drier is an efficient means of using it – more so than radiators or drying cabinets – but you have to take the high initial cost into consideration, and a wringer or spin drier *must* be used before the clothes go into the tumbler.

Freezers

These can be expensive white elephants. A freezer will save you money only if you work hard at it. Bulk buying of meat can save money, but the initial outlay is high, as mentioned in chapter 1, and, again, all the snags and temptations of bulk buying occur here.

Keep your freezer full. Why pay money to cool air? Bread is useful for filling up space, and purchases of butter, margarine, cheese, biscuits, sausages, bacon and other similar items which you may be able to buy at advantageous prices will all store successfully. If you have a garden, access to garden produce or 'pick-it-yourself' fruit, take full advantage, because there are real savings to be made here. Batch baking makes good use of the oven, and baking freezes well, as do casseroles and stews if you can be bothered making very large quantities. It may be that a freezer is more a convenience than a saving, especially for those at work. A lot depends on how much time you are prepared to spend and how much free or cheap produce is available to you.

Remember you have to spend some money on packaging materials, although extensive use can be made of ice cream and margarine containers, cream tubs and the foil containers used for carry-outs and ready-prepared meals. You will have to buy extra thick polythene bags and aluminium foil – it is possible to use the ordinary kind double, but this costs more. You will also need special freezer sealing tape. Group purchase of these items is well worth while, as bulk buying means a considerable saving.

In the event of a power cut, freezer owners follow one simple rule. On NO account open the freezer – you can open it 2-3 hours after it's all over. Food will stay frozen from 12-24 hours, depending on how fully loaded the freezer is. Electricity cuts seldom last that long. Ask about insurance as it does not always cover this particular contingency.

Dishwashers

These save time but, since both initial and running costs are high, there are undoubtedly cheaper ways of washing dishes. The dishwasher is often a pipe-dream of those who wash dishes on a regular basis, but before any sighs of regret are uttered, consider what it does not spare you. You still have to clear the table and scrape the dirty plates (quite the most unappealing aspect of the job anyway), load the dishes into the machine, and unload and put them all away. All that is saved is what is to me the best bit – the therapy of sloshing about in the hot suds! A quick rinse and drip dry and you have done the whole job much more cheaply. A few further labour-saving points: scrape and soak the dishes as soon as you clear them from the table; stand cutlery in a pan full of water – preferably hot. Try to wash pans before the meal. The soaking prevents food drying on, especially if washing up is delayed, and you will need less hot water as everything will be almost clean from the soak. Alternatively, issue each member of the family with his own mug, plate and irons and let them get on with it, each responsible for his own.

Dishwashers are neither a priority nor a necessity. Those who have them swear they could not live without them. Those without manage very well, and certainly save on hot water and things like salt and rinse-aid. In only one respect might a dishwasher save money, especially if you enlist the family's aid when washing up – there could be fewer breakages!

Floor polishers

There is an easy way to live without one of these. Have no polished floors. Make use of floor seals which can be used on almost every type of floor. Many polishers will also scrub a floor, but there are cheaper ways of doing this. The running cost of this piece of equipment is very low indeed, so the main consideration would be the initial outlay.

Small equipment
Mixers and blenders
A large mixer with all the attachments is a major buy. Contrary to the blandishments of advertisements, it is unlikely that the possession of such an instrument will turn you into a super cook, so don't count on this as any part of your investment. But if you enjoy home baking, and would do a lot more but for the time and effort involved, a mixer will help you save. Baking your own bread can be cheaper than buying; the same goes for cakes, scones and biscuits. I find a smaller model adequate for my own needs, and I could manage without it. A blender and grinder, on the other hand, is invaluable for making soups, breadcrumbs, purées and pancake batters.

These appliances are mainly time- and labour-saving. They do not, in themselves, actually save money though they may help indirectly.

Multicookers (electric frying pans)
An efficient use of electricity – you can cook a complete meal in one by the judicious use of aluminium foil as a separator. Two chickens can be roasted at once, and it is also possible to bake cakes. This is a versatile appliance which can cut down on fuel bills.

Infra-red grills
These are quite efficient as far as saving electricity is concerned – much more so than an 'open' grill, for example. They are messy to use and clean, and you would need a large one to cook for several people. They are good for cooking for one or two, and very useful where other facilities are limited – e.g. in a bed-sitter. The main snag, as with any type of grill, is the smoke and fumes.

Pressure cookers
Pressure cookers are great fuel- and time-savers, though it takes time for some people to overcome initial nervousness. They are a good buy since several foods can be cooked at the same time. And they are ideal for working families because of the much reduced cooking times.

Slow cookers

Expensive to buy but cheap to use, these might be purchased more for convenience than economy. The same end can be achieved by means of a much smaller outlay. An old-fashioned haybox or similar insulated container will serve the same purpose, and a modern version of this can be bought quite cheaply. Even more cheaply, a wide-necked Thermos can be used, and food will continue to cook in it for several hours. A stew, for example, after an initial 20-30 minutes on the stove, should be placed in the Thermos, which must be full to the top. Five hours later it will still be hot and the meat will be well-cooked. After a longer time, it may need to be reheated thoroughly.

Irons

You need an iron, and the extra cost entailed in the purchase of a steam iron, which does the job more efficiently, is well-justified. Use distilled water in it, or water which has been boiled, and empty it carefully after use, while it is still hot. Store standing on its heel to prevent corrosion of the sole plate. Some steam irons have a spray incorporated, which adds to the cost and though it is useful, you can do without it. If it clogs up – as it sometimes shows an unfortunate tendency to do – you will be without it anyway, or you must pay to have it cleared.

Toasters

Cheaper than using the grill, and a pop-up toaster will save money on burnt bread also!

Other small appliances

Many of the other small appliances like percolators, automatic tea-makers, electric blankets, carving knives, drills, hair driers and other gadgets should be considered in the same way as the foregoing appliances – they do make life easier and pleasanter, but could their function be fulfilled in a cheaper way, or do they really save time or money? If you are setting out to buy, think about how long it will take to recoup the initial outlay – only after that will you be saving, and then running costs and servicing must be taken into account.

Light bulbs

If light bulbs are the bane of your existence, there is one sure way of prolonging their life. Once you have placed a bulb in position, do *not* move it; or remove it. Dust it very gently if you must, but don't take it out to do so. Never move a bulb from a pendant, or hanging, position to a standing position in a table lamp, or vice versa. Bulbs do not respond to having their lives turned upside down and will soon let you know it by ceasing to function. 'Long life' bulbs simply give rather less light for a longer time.

Fluorescent tubes use less electricity. A 40 watt tube provides as much light as a 100 watt filament lamp. On the other hand, tubes are more expensive to replace, so in the long run there is little to choose between the two.

Care of new appliances

Some people seem to be dogged by misfortune in the purchase of electrical equipment. Whether it is entirely misfortune, and not due to some element of miscalculation, misinterpretation of instructions or simply misuse, is open to question. As one of the more fortunate mortals, with only three faulty appliances – two very minor – clocked up in twenty-odd years of buying consumer durables, it does seem to me that there must be more than luck to it. Too many rush into buying the wrong appliance for the purpose, and then proceed to use it in the wrong way. People can be frighteningly careless with expensive equipment for which they blithely pay over hard-earned money. Perhaps the anxiety of the older generation to look after things properly stems from the days when they were lucky to have anything to look after, but good care pays handsome dividends.

When you buy a new appliance the first essential is to sit down and READ THE INSTRUCTIONS. Never mind if it is the same as your last model, or Aunt Mary's – there may well be some crucial difference you should know about. Familiarize youself with all the knobs and switches, and all the DO's and DONT's. See that it is installed properly and wired correctly. If you can't do this, find someone who can. Most shops will put a plug on for you, but anyone can learn to do this (see p. 140). A modern three pin plug seems to demand the use of three hands, but one eventually learns to manage with two. The new wiring colour code must be mastered (see p. 139). If you get it wrong, one of three things will happen – the main fuse will blow, the appliance fuse will blow, or the appliance can remain live with the switch off – this last being the most dangerous, as the appliance will work and you may think all is well. Check very carefully, your life, or someone else's, could depend on it.

Instructions are given in order to ensure you enjoy the best possible result. The manufacturer *wants* you to get a good result. Don't wait till something goes wrong before you read instructions!

Keep appliances clean; a wipe over with a damp cloth, and an occasional polish will keep them like new. Little and often is much better than marathon sessions once a year, especially with cookers. Don't let spilled food and grease get burned on. Most appliances give details of any special care and cleaning required – follow them. See that the flex is kept in good repair; wind it carefully after use – kinks will fray, as will the parts which get most strain at the plug and where flex joins the appliance. Faulty flex can cause fire – don't risk it. Fires are expensive, so renew a worn flex promptly.

Servicing

There is much debate whether or not it pays to take out a service contract, which is really a kind of insurance. It is quite expensive as a rule, and a gamble. Only you can decide whether to take the risk. Remember you do have a guarantee for the first year and any fault should show up in that period. Always enquire about servicing when you buy and have appliances regularly serviced by qualified personnel. If the manufacturer is a member of AMDEA (Association of Manufacturers of Domestic Electrical Appliances) you will have the best chance of prompt attention, since there is a voluntary code of practice to which members adhere.

It refuses to work

If an appliance refuses to work, don't call for help immediately. You may be surprised to learn that about half the calls to service engineers are quite unnecessary – and therefore an expensive waste of money. Why pay someone several pounds to come out to switch on? It has happened!

Check:
Is the appliance switched on?
Is the main switch on?
Is the main circuit switch on?
Are the controls properly set?
Is the plug correctly wired?
Is the power on in the circuit or has the fuse gone? – Try plugging in another appliance to find out.

A gentle kick has been known to restore function, but is *not* recommended. You try it at your own risk. If you do aim a light blow and it works, the appliance has a faulty connection and you should seek out a qualified electrician.

Cooker

If there is any kind of bang or explosion, switch off at the main and get qualified help – quick! There is an emergency service (gas or electric), as I discovered when my cooker went off like a firework display – due to a short circuit when a pan boiled over. I was astounded when *two* men arrived within one hour of a call to the Electricity Board. Less spectacular faults are unlikely to command quite such speedy service, unfortunately.

Refrigerator and freezer

There is not much to go wrong. If the motor breaks down, you need specialized help. Under no circumstances open your freezer, unless it is to remove food to put it in someone else's. Food will usually stay frozen for 12-24 hours, depending on how full the freezer is and where it is situated. If a lot of expensive food is stored it should be insured against loss.

Washing machine

Refuses to empty	Very often due to a kink in the hose. Inspect and wiggle it gently in case the kink is in the bit of hose you can't see. (This happens with dishwashers too.)
Banging noises and vibration	Usually due to uneven balance of load when machine is spinning. Adjust the load evenly.
Overfoaming	Due to excess use of washing product. It may slow down, or even stop, the process. Clear by adding cold water and leaving for some time to allow froth to die down. If you can open the machine, remove articles, and as much foam as possible by hand.

Vacuum cleaner

Inefficient function probably means the bag needs emptying! A simple fault in all motor-driven appliances is a worn drive belt which is quite easy to replace. If the hose of a cylinder-type cleaner splits, a temporary repair can be made with plastic adhesive tape, insulating tape or masking tape. A blocked hose can sometimes be cleared by fitting it to the blowing end. Don't forget to put the other end of the hose in the suction end!

Discount buying

No one in their right mind pays the manufacturer's recommended price for anything. Limited sources of supply may force this upon you if you live in a remote area or buy mail order. This is an unfortunate fact of life. Not everyone realizes that all the rights accorded by the Sale of Goods Act (see pp. 157-8) also apply to discount buying. In a discount warehouse it is not always possible to examine your purchase as it is usually packed in its box, but open it up and inspect it if at all possible. It will save a lot of delay in the event of a superficial fault like a chip, dent, or loose or missing piece.

Shop around and try to plan your buys well in advance so that you can take advantage of sales and special offers.

Second hand

You can be very lucky, but it is a gamble. You must satisfy yourself that the equipment works. Age hasn't always much to do with usage; sometimes an article may be several years old and yet be little used. Equipment sold as 'reconditioned' is a different matter and very good value for money, especially when purchased from a reliable source. Often you can acquire two useful pieces of reconditioned equipment for the price of one brand new item.

chapter 5

HOUSEHOLD FURNISHINGS

The original purpose of furnishings was to provide warmth, comfort, and to satisfy our instinctive love of decoration. Today the criteria remain the same, though our standards of warmth and comfort are much higher, and decoration has become a very individual expression of status, personality and mood.

Savings certainly can be made in the provision of soft furnishings, curtains and linen, but it does mean less ambitious decorating schemes with an eye to simplicity, wearing qualities and flexibility of use. There is also a return to the workaday arts of repairing, cleaning and laundering, which should be learned and practised in order to make textile articles last and look good for as long as possible. The throw-away days of buy, use for a short time and then discard are receding steadily.

Soft furnishing fabrics

Soft furnishings are fabrics, and fabrics are composed of fibres. There is such a bewildering array on the modern market, that it is wise to know a little about the available range since a bad choice can prove both expensive and troublesome – particularly in the cleaning process, as will be seen in chapter 6.

Natural fibres

Cotton, linen, wool and silk have been used for many centuries. *Cotton* and *linen* are tough, hard-wearing and absorbent, but they crease easily and require ironing. Linen is very expensive to buy, but has a long life. *Wool* is resilient, dirt resistant, warm and expensive. It wears well but needs care in washing, and protection from moths. The use of *silk* in furnishings is certainly not for the budget-conscious, as it really is very much a luxury fabric.

Man-made fibres

The rayons, acetate and viscose, were the first of the man-made fibres, and the modern varieties, which now include Dicel, Tricel and Vincel, are a great improvement on these original 'art. silks'. They are very widely used in furnishings, particularly as curtain fabrics. Reasonably hard-wearing, they do need kind treatment in the wash tub.

Nylon and polyester include trade names like Enkalon, Celon, Perlon, Dacron, Crimplene, Terylene, Tergal. All wear and wash well, but may crease badly if wrongly handled. They dry very quickly which is a great advantage. Nylon tends to be weakened by sunlight, which accounts for the fact that there are few nylon curtains unless they have a bonded-on rayon lining. Polyester tends to absorb greasy stains which can be rather difficult to remove.

Acrylics – Acrilan, Orlon, Courtelle and Dralon are popular for household furnishings and linens, and are similar in wear and care to the last group, except in one important respect. They can stretch badly out of shape, permanently, if washed carelessly in water which is too hot.

Glass fibre is used for curtains, and though a little stiff, gives good service.

Plastic has become less popular, except for shower curtains. It tears relatively easily, and is prone to peculiar kinds of staining which are difficult, or impossible, to remove. It can also give off a distinctive smell.

Man-made and natural

One way to overcome disadvantages is by combining man-made with natural fibres, thus gaining the advantages of both. The most popular combination in the household linen market is *polyester and cotton*, widely used for bed linen.

Needs

Bed linen

No longer can it be said that you must have three pairs of sheets per bed (one on, one in the wash and one spare). It depends on the fabric, and whether or not you favour continental quilts. Nylon sheets will wash and dry in a day, and are remarkably cheap to buy. If you like them they are a real economy, in terms of wear, care, and the number required, but some people find them clammy, slippery and frankly unpleasant to sleep on. They also have an annoying tendency to pill (form tiny balls) on the surface. Try a pair for comfort – borrowed if possible – before you stock up with several pairs.

Polyester and cotton or vincel sheets are more expensive. The fabric is usually woven, not knitted which is the most common structure for nylon sheets. The cotton content in these blends makes them more absorbent and consequently more comfortable for those who dislike nylon. Quick-drying and minimum- or non-iron, they save both time and labour, but have the disadvantage of absorbing greasy stains – especially pillowcases. For this reason they should be washed often – and never buy white! It goes dingy looking in no time at all; coloured sheets will keep their appearance much longer. Patterns will disguise any general discolouration which gradually accumulates on pillowcases.

Cotton and linen are the traditional fabrics and are still popular. Flannelette or brushed cotton is cosy and needs little or no ironing. White cotton is still best for use if there is likely to be staining or a regular need for disinfection – hence its use in hospitals. It can also be a good buy for pillowcases, even if used with other types of sheet and certainly for under-pillowcases to protect your pillows. Linen is very expensive and needs ironing, certainly not an economy buy, though it will last almost forever.

Fitted sheets
These stay smooth and make bedmaking easier, but are not so flexible in use as flat ones which can be used either as top or bottom sheets, and on varying sizes of bed. Another disadvantage is that you cannot 'sides to middle' (see pp. 122-3.) fitted sheets very successfully.

Whether you are starting off anew, or just replacing linen, don't allow yourself to be dazzled by all the variety of colour and pattern available. It is wisest to choose colours and/or patterns which will fit happily in any room, as flexibility makes for more economy of use.

Blankets
Blankets were originally made of wool, or a mixture of wool and cotton. The loose crinkly wool fibres served to trap air which, strange as it may seem, is the reason for warmth. Wool is almost prohibitively expensive now and acrylic fibres are widely used for blankets – they are a little cheaper, though not quite so warm. They dry more quickly, however, have less tendency to shrink than wool, and are of no interest to moths. For these reasons, they may prove the better buy. Both types of fibre – wool and acrylic – can be made into cellular blankets which have an open 'holey' weave and are very lightweight.

They need another covering on top, to help trap the insulating air which provides the warmth. Cellular blankets are also obtainable in cotton – you may have noticed them on hospital beds – and they are excellent if frequent washing is required, as they will stand up to high temperatures and maximum wash processes. For children, invalids or bedridden people, these are a real economy buy.

There are cheaper alternatives to blankets. Travelling rugs cost less and are far more versatile. Admittedly they are smaller, but is it necessary to pay for extra amounts of expensive fabric just to tuck in? One large top cover is enough to keep all the others in place; or 'tuck in' strips of cheap fabric can be stitched along the sides – these strips could be the best parts of old blankets or sheets which have become worn in the middle.

Two old thin blankets can be stitched together by criss-cross lines of stitching. An interlining of some kind – old sheeting for example – will give added strength. You can also make a pretty top coverlet this way, by putting a coloured fabric on the outside, or by making a patchwork cover, which is not so ambitious as it sounds – patchwork can be done quite quickly with the sewing machine if you make patches on the large side. It is easy enough to collect scraps of cotton from outworn clothes and dressmakers' cuttings or samples. Check that colours are fast, or all your efforts may be ruined in the first wash!

An old army trick was to place newspapers between blankets for extra warmth. Mad, or distasteful, though this may sound, it worked. Again, the idea was to trap layers of air to act as insulation. Crumpled kitchen foil could serve the same purpose, and indeed a similar technique is used in survival kits. A useful point to remember is that a thin blanket, or two, placed *below* the bottom sheet can be very effective in keeping you warm.

Continental quilts

Since you never really make a bed again, they have much to recommend them! The initial cost is high, but no higher than the corresponding number of new blankets and coverlets. If you have lots of bed linen to use up, however, it will not be an economy to buy a continental quilt.

The 'warmth without weight' idea is once again due to trapped air – this time in down, feathers or a polyester filling. These quilts are altogether floppier than the conventional variety, and are meant to settle snugly round the sleeper. Some sleepers, unfortunately, never quite come to terms with them and this can result in a very expensive mistake. Try one before you buy. Certain firms will allow a trial for a few days, but failing this you could perhaps borrow one from friends to test for compatibility!

Real eiderdown filling is the most expensive, lightest and warmest; down and feather comes next, followed by feather and down – a subtle difference here! The first-mentioned in such combinations constitutes the highest proportion of filling – ask about this when buying. Feather alone is cheapest and quite satisfactory if you haven't known anything else!

Polyester in the form of Terylene or Dacron is also used for filling. This is slightly heavier but has the advantage of being washable and non-allergic. This type of filling is being constantly improved, and represents good value for money as it is significantly cheaper than down.

Kits are available so that you can make your own continental quilt, and these are widely advertised in the popular press. Handy people might like to try one – perhaps for a child's bed in the first instance. It is not wise to adapt an old quilt, as the feathers would need to be cleaned first to remove dust. Old feathers are also likely to have lost their air-trapping 'spring', packed as they are in a quilt, so the result might be disappointing unless done professionally, when more feathers will be added.

A continental quilt must have a separate cover to keep it fresh and stain-free. Covers are not cheap, and it is quite an economy to make one, though you need a lot of fabric. It has to withstand hard wear and constant washing, so there is not much point in looking around for the cheapest fabric you can find. You could be lucky and it *is* possible to save, but be sure that you are not expending time and effort on something which will not wear well. As you will need only a bottom sheet, if you are changing from sheets and blankets to a continental quilt, you could use a pair of sheets to make a cover. Plain white may lack appeal, but it can be dyed (see chapter 8). It is best to have a cover in a lightweight non-iron fabric, and if you want to make your own cover, cotton seersucker takes a bit of beating. It can be obtained in all colours and patterns, washes well and needs no ironing. Polyester and cotton can be bought by the metre, but it is likely to be more expensive than seersucker.

Making a cover is not difficult as it is simply a large bag. Be sure it is big enough (make a note of ready-made sizes) as the quilt must not be squashed up inside the enveloping cover. The fastening can be Velcro, zip, tape with press studs attached, or ordinary tying tapes. The last are cheapest but not so tidy looking.

Bedspreads

When considering bedspreads there are two points worthy of note: choose a cover which is washable and resistant to fading. There are many magnificent bed covers in the shops at equally magnificent prices. If the cost of regular dry cleaning has to be taken into the reckoning, then such covers are best ignored by those who seek economy. The familiar candlewick makes an admirable cover and is effective over a continental quilt, as it is heavy enough to drape well. The deep colours may fade quite badly in very sunny rooms, but can be re-dyed. Candlewick washes well and needs no ironing. Possibly the most practical and useful bedspread, if you can lay hands on one, was Grandma's favourite – the plain white heavy embossed cotton, sometimes termed 'Alhambra'. White goes with everything and is easiest of all to keep fresh and clean. White lace in cotton or man-made fabric comes a close runner-up. You can vary the effect with deep colours below and it too is easy to launder, though both require some ironing.

Quilts

The more conventional type of bed quilt has exactly the same range of fillings as continental quilts (p. 57), and prices vary according to filling in the same way. Polyester-filled quilts are washable – a useful attribute where children are concerned. Zip-up quilted sleeping bags are a good buy – they can be unzipped to use as bed quilts, and anything which serves a dual purpose is always an economy. If they get shabby in holiday use, remember they can go under a bed cover. Most are washable, but make sure of this when you buy.

Towels

You cannot do without towels. There is no real choice of fabric, towels being made almost exclusively of cotton because of its excellent qualities of absorbency. Very cheap towels are unlikely to wear well, as they are thin they will be less absorbent. On the other hand, the most expensive type often have very ornate patterns and special weaves which add to their cost, if not their effectiveness. Choose something between the two and look for a close weave (which will tighten further after the first wash) and strong hems. Deep colours may appear practical, but they get dirty just as quickly – it simply doesn't show so much! You could have problems with deep colours on washday as many are labelled 'wash separately'. This will mean more trouble and expense for you, so watch out for the warning tags.

You can almost dispense with tea towels by leaving dishes to drain, but a few are required for polishing up cutlery and glasses, and drying dishes when they are needed in a hurry. You can make tea towels from the best parts of old linen sheets or pillowcases; use double thickness if the material is very thin. Unbleached tea towels are a good buy, they are usually quite a bit cheaper and soon bleach in use.

Table linen

Do away with tablecloths altogether if you have a suitable table top, but there *are* some points in favour of table covers. Practical reasons are the protection of the table surface from heat, drips and splashes, and the deadening of noise. Cutlery and plates clattering on formica can make a nerve-racking din. (Remember school dinners!) And a cloth will conceal a well-worn table surface. The aesthetic advantages are that many of us enjoy setting an attractive table – it adds to the pleasure of eating the simplest food. You can also use varying colours of cloth which will create quite different effects with the same set of china. A cloth is cheaper than a dinner service, and unbreakable!

For family use, cotton seersucker wins – easy to wash and no ironing. Matching table napkins really do save stains on clothing. It is quicker and cheaper to wash tomato ketchup off a square of cotton than to have a suit cleaned.

If you want a grand cloth for entertaining, nylon or polyester lace are both attractive and easy to care for.

A white cotton or linen damask cloth needs careful ironing, but is quite the easiest to keep clean as you can boil, bleach, rub and scrub. The price of linen, new, is beyond what most people would be prepared to pay, but if you are really set on damask – and nothing looks more attractive on a festive table – it is often possible to buy one very cheaply second hand. They sometimes go at jumble sales for less than a pound. Elderly relatives may even have some tucked away, sad in the belief that no one wants them any more!

Place mats are useful, and much quicker and easier to launder than large cloths. You can easily choose the wipe-clean variety which saves any laundering at all. Traycloths are little used, as many modern trays have surfaces which make the use of a cloth superfluous. However, if a tray is to be used for meals in bed, a cloth makes things easier by preventing the plates from skidding about alarmingly.

Window coverings

The usual choice lies between curtains and blinds and they are used for a number of reasons, the main ones being warmth, privacy, decoration and the protection of carpets and furniture from strong sunlight.

Blinds

Blinds are used for privacy and protection from sun. Decoration is a secondary function, and they are not so warm as thick curtains. Most blinds will outlast several pairs of curtains and for this reason may prove a better buy, even if the initial cost is higher. They are easier to look after and less likely to fade. The range varies from cheap paper blinds to expensive slatted blinds.

Roller blinds

Paper blinds are useful and inexpensive – ideal if you need a simple short-term window covering. They are also good for a spare bedroom, although if the blind is to be used to keep sun out it will get a fair amount of wear, if privacy is the main factor there will not be nearly so much use. Roller blinds can be made of almost any fabric and are usually treated to make them resistant to dirt and spongeable. Patterns and colours abound, but choose something which will not tie you too much should you wish to change the colour scheme of the room.

Slatted blinds

Usually known as 'Venetian', the slats may be vertical or horizontal. They are more expensive than other types of blind and should be looked on as a long-term investment, so choose a fairly neutral colour which will adapt to a change of colour scheme. It is unlikely that they will remove successfully to another house, though it can sometimes come about. The great advantage of slatted blinds is that they afford both privacy and sun shading without constant pulling up and down. In a very sunny house they are well worth their cost in the saving to carpets, upholstery and furniture, particularly if you are out all day and do not wish to advertise the fact by leaving your curtains closed. The blinds themselves do not fade, as they are made of painted aluminium or plastic. They have one major disadvantage – they are hell to clean!

Regular dusting with the brush attachment of the vacuum cleaner helps, but sooner or later you have to wash them. The bath is sometimes recommended, but you could scratch it badly, and the wet slats cling together tenaciously. The best way is to lay the blind flat on the ground, opened, over a large piece of polythene or an old sheet, and get down on your knees to wash it, first one side then the other. After trying everything I find this the easiest way. Use liquid detergent or Flash if the slats are very dirty, as these products do away with rinsing and they also avoid streaks. Vertical blinds are made of specially stiffened fabric which can be wiped clean. Since they can be taken down a slat at a time, this makes the job much easier, as anyone who has battled with a giant Venetian blind will appreciate!

Blinds save money in another way – they make it unnecessary to have curtains at all. If you feel the room looks a bit bare without, a narrow decorative curtain hung at either side is much less expensive than the amount of fabric needed to draw across the whole window. Blinds help to keep the room warm by trapping an insulating layer of air between themselves and the glass.

Curtains

Thick curtains do keep a room warm, and lining improves the insulation still further. Other functions are mainly to provide decoration and privacy. Buying curtains can make a big hole in the budget, but there are ways to cut the cost. If you want curtains to last for a long time, buy a fabric which is shrink-and fade-resistant. It may cost more but it is well worth it. 'Dry clean only' is a warning to steer clear if you hope to save money.

Curtain lining is almost as dear as the curtain fabric, but it makes the curtains heavier and protects them from strong sun. (A blind may be a better choice than lining, if protection from sun is important.) If you have old thin curtains of a suitable size and colour, you could use these as lining.

Net curtains are used for privacy and also to give some screening from strong sunlight. They are usually made of

Terylene polyester or cotton. The former needs frequent washing, especially in city atmospheres.

New curtains the cheap way

The cheapest way to have new curtains is to make them yourself. This is not at all difficult except for the pattern matching and calculation. There are two ways round this difficulty. Buy a self-coloured fabric or one where the pattern requires only very simple matching, e.g. vertical stripes. Or ask nicely in the shop! A helpful assistant – and there are still a good many of them – will often cut, or at least mark the required lengths for you. Always go to the shop with accurate window measurements, including the height and position of the rail. A point of economy to bear in mind is that if you choose a pattern with a big drop you will have to buy quite a lot of extra fabric to accommodate the pattern in full, which could involve you in a great deal of extra expense. Check this carefully before having any fabric cut in the shop. Gain experience on small curtains in a cheap fabric for kitchen or bathroom. Once you know what you are doing you can embark on larger and more expensive ones.

Rufflette publish an excellent booklet on curtain making which gives much more detail than is possible here but the main essentials are as follows.

Quantity of fabric

All curtain fabric is liable to shrinkage, sometimes by quite a startling amount. This must be allowed for in calculation, and though shrink-resist fabric is a good buy, it pays to play safe with it too. You need *at least* $1\frac{1}{2}$ times the width of the curtain rail; twice as much is better; and if you want to use one of the pleated heading tapes $2\frac{1}{2}$-3 times as much (this is *not* an economy and the special tape is expensive also, but what you save by your DIY effort might justify the cost). The length should be 20 cm (8 in) more than the distance from rail to finished level, which may be either floor or sill. If you have central heating radiators below the window choose sill length, otherwise you will trap all the heat behind the curtain, and possibly damage the fabric as well. Decide how much money you will spend, and choose a fabric which enables you to have a generous width of curtain within that price. A skimped amount of expensive material will only give a disappointing result – it is better to buy something cheaper which allows for more luxurious draping.

Making curtains and linings

Making up curtains is quite simple, but you do need use of a
sewing machine. Match the pattern carefully and join the
required number of widths, using matching thread suitable for
the type of fabric. Puckered seams can ruin the appearance of
curtains, so check machine tension carefully and either cut off
selvedges, or snip them at intervals to release the pull. Press
seams carefully after stitching. Finish the sides with neat hems.
Heavy fabrics look better with hand slip-stitched hems – it is
not as laborious as it sounds, since the stitches can be fairly far
apart. The curtains will look more professional than professional ones, which always seem to have all the hems machine
stitched.

The next step is to apply heading tape (the standard variety)
– a simple enough operation. Fold over the top raw edge of the
curtain 4 cm (1½ in) and tack. Prepare the tape by pulling out
4 cm (1½ in) of the cords at one end and knot them together.
Cut off the extra tape. Pull out 5 cm (2 in) of cord at the opposite end for pleating. Turn the ends of the tape under,
enclosing the knotted cords under one end. Pin or tack the tape
to the curtain, covering the raw edge and leaving about 2½ cm
(1 in) between the top edge of the curtain and the top edge of
the tape. Stitch all round outer edge – outside the cords. The
last operation is the hem at the lower edge and it is a good idea
to let the curtains hang for a day or two before you do this, as
the weight of the fabric may cause it to drop a little. If you have
allowed a good deal of fabric for shrinkage – on floor length
curtains, for example – you can turn a double hem rather than
make a very deep one. Hand hemming is again infinitely preferable in my estimation – it looks better, is much easier to
unpick and leaves no mark if you have to adjust the hem at a
later date. Pull cords are available to match the curtain track
and are worth the money as they save wear and tear on your
curtains. Remember to change curtains from left to right
annually as this also saves constant wear and fading in the same
place.

Linings are made up in a similar way to curtains. Use
special lining tape and *never* stitch the lining permanently to
the curtains. It leads to endless problems in washing and cleaning as the fabrics can shrink by different amounts, and you
cannot change the linings from one pair of curtains to another
if you want to use lighter curtains in summer. The same lining
can be used on different curtains – a useful economy. In a city

the linings will probably get dirty before the curtains as they are nearest the outside and form a sort of filter for fumes and dirt. It is very convenient to be able to wash linings separately and more frequently.

Loose covers

The main purpose of loose covers is either to protect an upholstered piece of furniture, or to refurbish its shabby appearance. Buying fabric loose covers means having them made to measure and is a very expensive undertaking. To make them yourself is an ambitious project, but not impossible if you have the required amount of patience and skill. It far exceeds the demands of curtain making, however, and should not be attempted unless you are quite confident or have expert advice available. It is still expensive to make them yourself and your time and effort should not be wasted on cheap fabric. In the long run it might well prove a sounder investment to have the furniture re-upholstered in a hard-wearing material. Loose covers wear, fade and require frequent washing.

A good alternative are stretch-type loose covers in man-made fibre. They look attractive and give good value for money. They wear well, though the fabric is prone to catch on sharp objects like claws on rings (and pets) and they can melt under a cigarette burn. The fabric washes easily, needs no ironing and is quick-drying.

Cheap brighteners

If any kind of re-curtaining or re-covering is outwith your means there is an inexpensive way of giving your room a lift. Make some brightly coloured cushion covers – they catch the eye and thus detract from the effect of wear and tear elsewhere! Chairbacks can either prevent or cover up wear and stains. You can simply fringe the edges of any suitable fabric, or be as ambitious as you like with embroidery or crochet. Re-covering a lampshade is not difficult and new cushion covers, chairbacks and lampshades will give any room a new look for a very small outlay – perhaps none, if you have any leftover fabric from dressmaking or curtains.

Care and storage of linen and furnishings

Care involves laundering which is fully covered in chapter 6, while mending, patching and other repairs are illustrated in chapter 10.

Storage

Storage is very often too casual, resulting in deterioration or even damage, so it is worth giving some careful thought to this. If your linen cupboard is shared by your hot water cylinder, then the cupboard is really meant for airing. Things like towels, sheets and pillowcases can be stored therein if they are in regular use, but it is not a good place for long-term storage of seldom used linens, as the warmth can cause yellowing. A drawer, cupboard, trunk or even a box in a cooler spot is much better. Keep old thin pillowcases to put things in.

Air things well before storing, or mildew may result. This dread fungus actually grows on damp fabric and is very difficult to eradicate (see Stain Removal Guide p. 91) so is always best avoided. If blankets or curtains are being stored during summer, wash or clean them before storing, and use a moth preventative on, near, or around blankets if they are made of wool. Curtains and blankets can be kept in polythene bags. The ironing of curtains should always be left until you want to put them up again. Velvet curtains – if you are so lucky – are best rolled. The fabric department of a store will usually let you have empty cardboard rolls which are ideal for the purpose. If you have to fold velvet curtains to store, place tissue paper between the folds.

Sales

Sales offer excellent opportunities to purchase household linens of all kinds, but map out your needs well in advance and be quite sure about the sizes and colours which will fulfil these needs. Remember that 'seconds' are likely to have small flaws or faults so look for these and satisfy yourself that you can either ignore or repair them. Odd sizes and colours and broken sets or discontinued ranges offer very good value.

Curtain material is often greatly reduced and you can usually find something to suit your needs. There are bargains in ready-made curtains too, if you have no sewing machine – or no time.

Look out for 'special offers' in re-upholstering, this is a real chance to renew your furniture if normal prices floor you. Blinds can also be obtained at big discounts.

Second hand

Curtains are the most likely soft furnishings to be found in the small ads. Country auction sales, job lot auctions and jumble sales make good hunting grounds, but be sure you know what you are buying, as there is an element of risk. Good quality velvet or velour curtains will re-dye successfully if they are slightly faded, though this is not a job to be attempted at home. Provided you can buy the curtains at a price which is reasonable to you, it is worth spending the few extra pounds on renewing their appearance.

Beautiful table linen can be acquired more easily second hand than new, since the painstaking hand embroidery and crochet of the last few generations have now almost ceased to exist as crafts. A large lace table cloth can make a magnificent bed cover. Often the linen on view at sales is stained or discoloured, but provided it is white, it is almost certain that most of the staining can be removed (see chapter 7), so don't be too easily put off. If the idea of regularly laundering such items makes you shudder, you had best avoid them, but remember small pieces can be permanently mounted under glass table tops, which gives individuality yet saves laundering time.

The same points apply to bed linen. Watch out for signs of moth (holes!) in blankets. Consider other possibilities for worn bed linen (see p. 125) if it is going for a song. It could save money in other ways.

chapter 6

LAUNDRY

Modern laundry is complicated. Technology has taken away much of the back-breaking labour, but presents us with a different set of problems. New fabrics, washing products and machines must be properly and carefully used if good results are to be obtained. Cavalier attitudes to washday simply lead to costly and avoidable mistakes. Not everyone appreciates this, as is evident from the number of consumer complaints about textile articles. A great deal of money could be saved in many homes by spending a little more care and attention on washday.

Everyone has to wash clothes. It is a chore which is inevitable. Commercial laundry prices are far beyond the pockets of the budget-conscious, and anyway their results can be disappointing. The term 'easy-care' is often used to describe modern fabrics. It is rather misleading, and is often interpreted as meaning NO care required. Ironically, these are often the fabrics which need quite a lot of care if you are going to get best results.

The whole aim in washing is to remove soiling and to restore, as far as possible, the original appearance of the article. This is not difficult, and it is not hard work, but it does take some planning and, consequently, a little more time. The choice is yours, but the small amount of extra time taken can pay handsome dividends in the length of useful life of your clothes and furnishings.

Care labels

There is one valuable guide through the technological maze of washday, and that is the British Care Labelling Scheme. This was designed by the Home Laundering Consultative Council, a body representing most of the industries concerned with textiles, detergents and laundry equipment, in addition to distributors, label manufacturers, commercial launderers and cleaners, and educational and consumer interests. The highly successful labelling scheme is widely recognized though un-

and in my experience the results have been satisfactory. On dark coloured fabrics, it is best to sprinkle powder on the wrong side.

Lubricants

Many stains can be removed from washable fabrics by treating with liquid detergent, washing-up liquid or Swarfega. Gently rub in neat liquid, leave for a short time, then wash in the usual way. Glycerine used to be recommended, but the first-mentioned have a similar effect and you are more likely to have washing-up liquid to hand. Liquid soap can also be used, i.e., the jelly from the underside of a bar of soap.

Stain Removal Guide

Adhesives

Ordinary gum can be removed with warm water. Other types of adhesive may respond to acetone or spirit cleaner. Some manufacturers supply suitable solvents for their products. A rough guide is to use spirit cleaner on opaque adhesives, and acetone on the clear ones.

Alcohol

Blot up immediately. (Soak a table cover in cool water.)

Washables Usually the stain will wash out. Use liquid detergent neat on a red wine stain. Or use an absorbent. If the stain persists try a suitable bleach.

Non-washables Sponge with cool water and liquid detergent. If stain persists try hydrogen peroxide. Absorbent on fine fabrics.

Blood

Washables Soak in biological or non-soapy detergent or cool water (NEVER hot – the stain will set) then wash at maximum safe temperature for fabric. Use colour remover if stain persists, or a solution of ammonia and water: 1 teaspoon ammonia to $\frac{1}{2}$ litre (1 pint) water.

Non-washables Sponge with cool water and liquid detergent. A really bad stain must be treated professionally.

Candle wax

Scrape off as much as possible. Remove remainder with a warm iron over blotting paper. Use a grease solvent on any residual mark.

Chewing gum

Use a grease solvent. An ice cube will harden the gum until it is brittle enough to scrape off strong fabrics.

Chocolate/Cocoa

Scrape off as much as possible.

Washables Treat with liquid detergent, then wash in usual way. If stain persists, try suitable bleach.

Non-washables Sponge with liquid detergent. If this fails treat with grease solvent or an absorbent.

Cod liver oil

Washables Rub in liquid detergent then wash in hottest water possible.

Non-washables Treat with grease solvent or an absorbent.

Note: difficult stain to remove. Avoid it by giving child cod liver oil whilst in the bath – or give in capsule form.

Coffee

Washables Soak in non-soapy or biological product or treat with liquid detergent. Wash in usual way. Bleach any residual stain.

Non-washables Sponge a fresh stain or use an absorbent if this fails or hydrogen peroxide.

Cream

Washables Liquid detergent followed by washing.

Non-washables Treat with grease solvent or an absorbent.

Creosote

Use benzene or lighter fuel as a solvent. Note: These are highly inflammable. Use with great care.

Curry

Must be treated immediately, or at least kept wet.

All fabrics Use liquid detergent. Try suitable bleach if stain persists.

Dye

Washables Use colour remover or bleach.

Non-washables Damp and sprinkle with colour remover. This is risky so test carefully. Sponge thoroughly to rinse.

Egg *see* Blood

Emulsion paint

Washables Rinse thoroughly. A dry stain is almost impossible to remove, but try acetone.

Non-washables Sponge fresh stain. A dry stain, as above.

Fruit juice

Washables Soak in non-soapy or biological product, or treat with liquid detergent, then wash. Or soak fresh stain in bicarbonate of soda.

Non-washables Sponge; try absorbent on fine fabrics. Treat residual colour with suitable bleach.

Grass
All fabrics Treat with methylated spirit.

Gravy
Washables Soak in a non-soapy or biological product. Wash in usual way.
Non-washables Sponge; use grease solvent or an absorbent.

Grease
Washables Treat with liquid detergent. Wash in hottest water possible with solvent detergent. Use grease solvent if stain persists.
Non-washables Use grease solvent or an absorbent.

Ink: Biro
All fabrics Treat with liquid detergent or methylated spirit.

Writing
All fabrics Sponge out washable ink. Use lemon juice on permanent ink.

Red ink
All fabrics Sponge with vinegar. Rinse.

Felt pens
These vary in content. Try cold water first.
Washables Liquid detergent. Use suitable bleach if stain persists.
Non-washables Methylated spirit, grease solvent, or acetone.

Make-up (lipstick, face cream, eye make-up)
Washables Treat with liquid detergent; wash in usual way with solvent detergent.
Non-washables Grease solvent.

Mildew
Washables Launder and allow to dry in the sun. If this fails use suitable bleach.
Non-washables Professional help required.

Milk
Washables Soak in non-soapy or biological product or plain cool water – *never* hot, as the stain will set permanently.
Non-washables Sponge with cool water.

Mud
Washables Allow to dry, brush well. If stain persists it will usually wash out.
Non-washables After brushing treat with grease solvent.

Nail varnish
All fabrics Nail varnish remover or acetone. Test with extra care, especially on acetate, Tricel and polyester (Terylene, Dacron, etc.) – amyl acetate is a safer solvent, but not foolproof.

Orange juice *see* Fruit juice

Paint

All fabrics Treat with suitable paint solvent, e.g. Polyclens or turpentine. A dried stain requires patience to loosen it. Place a pad soaked in solvent over the stain for 30 minutes, then apply more solvent. Alternate solvent with liquid detergent. When stain is removed, sponge with warm water. An expensive garment is best treated professionally.

Perspiration

Washables Soak in biological or non-soapy detergent and warm water. Wash in usual way.

Non-washables Sponge with above solution.

If white fabric is discoloured with perspiration, use a suitable bleach. Dye which has been affected can sometimes be improved by sponging or soaking with household ammonia diluted with an equal quantity of water. Use this on a fresh stain. Vinegar is used on an old stain. If this treatment is not effective there is nothing else you can do.

Rust

Use a proprietary rust remover, like Movol, which can be bought at a chemist's. Note: Rust stains can spread on wet fabric so don't put a rust-stained article in the general wash. Bleach may cause a hole.

Scorch

Use a suitable bleach on cotton and linen fabrics. (Man-made fabrics will not scorch – they melt!) Heavy fabrics can be rubbed lightly with very fine grade sandpaper, an emery board or a silver coin. If this fails, use hydrogen peroxide.

Shoe polish

All fabrics Use grease solvent.

Soft drinks *see* Fruit juice

Soot/smoke

Washables Use a solvent detergent. Soak and wash as usual.

Non-washables Grease solvent or an absorbent.

Tar

All fabrics Eucalyptus oil followed by grease solvent.

Tea *see* Coffee

Urine

Washables Soak in biological or non-soapy detergent. Wash in usual way.

Non-washables Blot up as much as possible. Sponge several times with cool water. If colour seems affected, sponge with vinegar solution: 1 tablespoon vinegar to 4 tablespoons water.

Yellowing and discolouration

White cottons and linens (without special finish)

Soak in a heavy duty wash product. Give wash code 1 high temperature wash and boil if possible. They could also be bleached outside in the sun, or with household bleach.

Nylon

Proprietary nylon whitener could be tried but it is more practical to dye the article a deep colour.

Polyesters (Terylene, Crimplene, etc.)

Proprietary whitener. Household bleach can sometimes be as effective, but test to make sure. It is good for net curtains, but some polyesters may turn yellow.

Acrylic fibres

Soak in heavy duty detergent. Household bleach may also be effective on acrylics.

Elastic fibres

Nothing is particularly effective on these.

Wool

Proprietary whiteners are effective. Hydrogen peroxide can also be used.

Note: If buying a proprietary whitener (which is really a fluorescent dye), make sure it is the right one for the fabric you want to treat.

Emergencies

If you spill something – immediately scrape, soak or blot up as much as possible. Food and blood stains should be soaked right away in cold water. Even if you think the fabric may water-mark, it will be easier for you or the dry cleaner to get rid of that than a set-in stain. A greasy stain – or indeed anything which is unaffected by water – like paint, biro ink or tar – must be treated with an appropriate solvent as soon as possible.

Old, unknown stains

Washable fabrics could be treated with liquid detergent and washed. If this fails, try soaking for 30 minutes (or longer) in biological or non-soapy product. The last resort is to try a suitable bleach. If this fails, give up!

On non-washables, assuming the fabric is suitable, first sponge with cool water. If the stain remains when dry, use a grease solvent. Try a paste of fuller's earth and spirit cleaner. Allow this to dry, then brush off. Repeat if there is an improvement. The last resort is suitable bleach – or a patch.

chapter 8

HOME DYEING

This is a way of practising economy which really is fun. The initial outlay is not great and the dividends in terms of job satisfaction and money saving are both high. Unlike gardening and painting (which are both slow to show results and strenuous in the execution) this is a quick, easy and spectacular way of working magic. Flexibility is the secret of economic survival.

Being human, and members of a consumer society which conditions us to want new things, we often hanker after a change in our clothes and surroundings. Textile articles are very expensive to replace but dyeing can completely transform them, extending and even altering their potential uses. No one wants white sheets for window curtains, but sheets dyed to tone with other furnishings acquire a completely new look. Dyed sheeting can also be used for making garments, and you may well possess redundant cotton sheets if you have changed over to continental quilts or to nylon or polyester and cotton for easier laundering.

Clothes change character completely: colour co-ordinated outfits can be produced from odd garments which might otherwise be discarded. Once the enthusiasm is generated, it may be carried on to gloves, bags, shoes and other accessories. Something apparently new for a very small outlay is an economy to appeal to everyone, and the craft of dyeing is really enjoyable. The artistic will find outlet for their talents in experimenting with paint-on dyes, tie-and-dye techniques and batik, but even those who limit creation to a set of new scarlet underwear will undoubtedly feel pleased with their efforts.

Limitations

Magic though the effects may be, there is more to dyeing than waving a wand. There are limitations and these should be fully appreciated to avoid disappointing results.

Fabric

Most fibres can be successfully dyed at home, with the exception of Acrilan, Orlon and Courtelle, which will not come to any harm, but they all resist absorption of the dye solution. Polyester is not a howling success either. Special finishes such as drip dry, flameproof, waterproof and pleated articles are best avoided as are cashmere, angora, mohair and anything with a foam backing or bonded lining. Fibres soak up dye at different rates, and this can produce interesting – if unexpected – effects. A cotton garment with nylon trimming will come out two-tone but none the worse for that. Buttons and stitching may produce similar results, and so will a lining of different fibre content.

What to dye

Almost anything provided it is washable. Starting with underwear, you can turn dingy-looking white nylon into bright clear colours. Don't make the mistake of choosing pale pastel dyes – gloomy white will just become gloomy pink. Shirts, blouses, dresses, nightwear and woollies, household linens (you can achieve great things with jumble sale or other bargain buys), sheets, pillowcases, towels and tablecloths are all suitable, and cotton and linen damask give a particularly attractive result. Lightweight curtains and bedcovers and single woollen blankets are also possibilities, but large and heavy articles like velvet curtains and extra thick candlewick bedspreads may be better dyed professionally, or perhaps at the launderette. You need a lot of dye and a large container, and it is often cheaper to send heavy items away to be done, especially if they are of good quality with lots of wear left in them.

Before you begin

There are some pitfalls which you should know about. Stains and fading will not miraculously disappear; unfortunately, they will probably look worse. Articles must be carefully examined for stains, which should be removed before you begin. Perspiration staining may not be apparent on a white or light coloured article, but will show up to a disfiguring extent after dyeing, so it is wise to soak garments in a biological wash product to eliminate this hazard. A dye-stripper or colour remover must be used on faded articles to get the whole fabric reduced to the same colour level. This will not work on fast coloured articles, so test a small piece of fabric first, before buying a large amount of colour remover. The same procedure must be employed if you want to dye a dark coloured article a lighter colour. This is not always successful and better avoided. It is always easier to over-dye a dark colour in a deeper shade. Make use of the 'starting' colour and remember that it will always affect the finished result.

Colour guide

Fabric colour	Dye	Result
Red	Yellow	Scarlet
Red	Blue	Purple
Blue	Yellow	Green
Pale blue	Pink	Lavender
Yellow	Pink	Coral
Green	Brown	Olive
Purple	Yellow	Light brown
Orange	Pink	Coral

Dyeing black is difficult and the result may depress you by turning out dirty charcoal grey. You can try again, using more black dye, but if you are willing to settle for any other colour, do so. Patterned fabrics can be over-dyed very successfully, but remember that 'colour arithmetic' will also apply in the varying shades obtained in the result.

Choosing a dye

The first thing to do is weigh the article. If you have no scales refer to the table of weights (p. 78), although this is only an approximate guide. It is important to have *enough* dye, and this has nothing to do with the amount of liquid in the dye bath. You will not make the colour paler by adding more water or darker with less. It all depends on the proportion of fabric to dye powder.

Buy the right quantity of dye, and one which is suitable for the fabric – it will give this information on the container. It is not always easy to identify the fabric – look for a label. If there isn't one, you will have to guess and accept the risk if you have guessed wrongly, or choose a multi-purpose dye. There are several types of dye on the market, and all are easy to use. Success is dependent on following the detailed instructions given (boring repetition, but indisputable fact!).

Multi-purpose dyes

These are sold in both powder and liquid form and are suitable for all natural and most synthetic fabrics. The liquid has the advantage that it is ready mixed and you only use what you need. It also makes mixing and matching colours easier.

Detergent/Dyes

These combine washing and dyeing in the same process, making the dyeing of large articles very simple by cutting out the pre-wash required. They can be used – and are sometimes available – in most launderettes. They are suitable for most fabrics, but the articles should not be very heavily soiled, and any grease stains must first be removed. These dyes are usually used in a washing machine.

Cold water dyes

These are extra-permanent, and suitable only for natural fibres – cotton, linen, wool, viscose rayon and silk. Household salt and washing soda are both used to deepen and fix colour, or you can buy special fixative. Since the colour is extra-permanent, it is wise to wear rubber gloves when working. You do not require to boil or heat up articles when using this method.

Method

For some fabrics the type of dye you select will depend on what facilities you have available.

Sink, bath, plastic bucket – Obviously you cannot apply heat to any of these, but they are fine for cold water dyeing, or tinting with hot dyes. In the latter case use the hottest water possible, but expect to get pale shades only.

Wash boilers and twin tub washing machines – are suitable for all methods. Protect the inside of the lid with cooking foil.

Automatic washing machines – are suitable for all hot dyes (including detergent/dyes) but some cannot be used with cold dyes. You may find this information in your instruction book, or you can write to the dye manufacturers – most have a consumer adviser.

Pans, metal buckets or enamel basins – All these can be successfully used on top of the stove.

Note: It is vitally important that there is *plenty of room* for the articles to move around freely in the dye. In a washing machine never use more than half capacity, e.g. $1\frac{1}{2}$ kg (3 lb) if machine tub will hold 3 kg (6 lb). If articles are squashed together, the result will be patchy and uneven.

General points on procedure

Detailed instructions will be provided with whatever dye you purchase, and these must be carefully followed, but some extra hints may prove useful. Do not start a dyeing session unless you have colour remover handy. The articles to be dyed must be clean, wet, free from stains and washing powder, i.e. thoroughly rinsed. Dissolve the dye according to instructions. Be careful not to spill powder on work surfaces or wet articles – it tends to get around! Prepare the dye bath and immerse the articles, well opened out. If you are using an automatic washing machine you can now go off and have a cup of tea, but with any other method you must stick around to stir, if you want a good result.

It is better not to use the agitator or pulsator in a twin tub machine, unless you can have a 15 minute cycle. Repeating a 4 minute pulsator wash 4 times puts unnecessary strain on the fabric. It is better just to use the heater (if required) and stir by hand. This is essential for wool, which may shrink if agitated too much. Gradually raise the temperature to that recommended for the fabric in the case of hot water dyes. Don't try to cut the timing in any method. Fibres need time to absorb dye completely, otherwise the result will be less permanent. Be sure you complete any fixing processes required.

When dyeing is completed, rinse, rinse, rinse, and rinse again until the water is clear. Do NOT rinse in the spin drier, as this may result in streaks and spots. The rinsing process clears away any loose dye from the surface of the fabric. If you do see some minor streakiness on things like nylon undies, try rubbing them with soap; this will often remove the excess dye. Dry articles in the usual way.

The first time you wash dyed articles, it is wise to do them on their own, as the cleansing action of your washing powder may remove a little of the dye. Any dye which inadvertently transfers itself to other fabrics can be removed with bleach or colour remover. Flush out the boiler, washing machine or whatever receptacle you have used with a solution of bleach.

A quick trick, if you only want temporary pastel shades, is to dip articles in the dye solution in the kitchen sink and swish them around for about 15 minutes. Shadow effects can be created by keeping some parts in longer than others.

To match colours

You may wish to dye one article to match another. The best

way of doing this is by making a test piece to start with. Cut a tiny piece off the hem or seam of both articles, and wet these. Do not put all the dye in the dye bath at once. Add a little at a time until you get the test piece to the shade matching your (*wet*) original. Now the whole article may be placed in the dye bath until it too becomes the desired shade. You will probably have to add a little more dye, but try it without first. Lift the article out before making any additions to avoid streaks or splotches of dye.

The same technique is used when you have to mix two dyes to obtain a particular colour.

Unexpected results

Never start dyeing unless you have a tin of colour remover handy. Ordinary household bleach is often effective, but slower. If the result of your dyeing is patchy, unexpected, or hideous, use colour remover right away and start afresh. You may also need bleach if you spill dye. Sometimes it is possible to over-dye hideous colour – say, a violently repulsive yellow – with a darker shade, so consider this before stripping the unwanted colour.

Other dyeing possibilities

Carpets can be successfully dyed at home. It is quite an undertaking, as the dye is actually brushed on and it must be done carefully, but it is certainly a way of refurbishing a room by changing the look of a carpet which may have years of useful life left, though the colour is unsuitable. Experiment on a small piece and see whether you like the effect. This procedure opens up possibilities for second-hand carpets too, but do remember, as with other dyed articles, fading, wear and stains will not disappear. You could paint or stencil a design in a darker shade to disguise stains and fading, although this would only be a possibility on a self-coloured carpet.

Lampshades can be dyed, so can canework (wet it first then paint on dye), straw articles like table mats, faded plastic flowers, rope, string, feathers and dried grasses. Brightening up your home becomes a really economical proposition.

Paint-on dyes can be used on fabric to give patterned effects which will go happily into the wash tub. Paint-on shoe colour can also be used to renew the appearance of luggage and shopping bags. This paint-on colour can be used on vinyl surfaces as well as leather, and it does not matter what shade is underneath. Suede dye is paint-on also, but as with fabric dyes, the ground colour will affect the result, as this dye soaks into the suede. It can be used on boots, shoes, bags, belts and gloves. Clean them thoroughly with suede cleaner first. Two applications of colour are usually required. Allow to dry after each application and brush up the nap before applying a second coat.

Tie-dye and batik are crafts which the enthusiastic dyer may well wish to pursue, as beautiful patterned effects in more than one colour can be obtained. Their scope is too wide for this book, but dye manufacturers publish excellent leaflets on all aspects of dyeing, many of them free of charge. If you cannot obtain these, your local library will be able to help.

Good craft work is always in demand, and those with the interest and skill might find in this a new possiblity of supplementing their income as well as making the most of existing resources.

Economy note
You are likely to get carried away with your new power! Don't *waste* money by dyeing articles just for the fun of it. The dyes themselves are not cheap, so keep your enthusiasm for things which will be substantially improved by a colour change. If it is a case of 'using up the dye' you may certainly treat the men in your life to purple pants.

chapter 9

FAMILY CLOTHING

Social custom decrees that we cover our nakedness – though the tradition must stem from necessity as much as from convention in the rigours of the British climate! We need warm clothing for winter, waterproof clothing for wet weather and lighter, which usually means cheaper, garb for summer. We also wear clothes to enhance (or disguise!) appearance and to express personality. And for the latter reason most of us probably have far more than we need.

Clothes

Clothes may be a particularly important part of a life style – children may need school uniform, for example, and certain types of employment may dictate a particular standard of dress, so that money for clothes assumes a degree of priority. It is important to keep up appearances. One can be smartly dressed today on a very limited budget indeed, particularly if clothes are well cared for. It is too easy to overdo 'anti-consumer' attitudes to the extent of slouching around in tatty jeans and sweaters all the time. Jaded sweaters can be covered by cheaper, attractive shirts or smocks. Protective clothing, which is less expensive than new heavier winter clothes, is available in all styles and sizes. This enables you to get the maximum wear from things which are past their best. Learn the useful arts of mending, strengthening and repairing, and if you have not yet made an attempt to master the crafts of knitting and sewing, the time is ripe for experiment. This is an area where considerable economies can be made, particularly if you have time at your disposal.

Quantity

In the pursuit of economy, obviously, get by with as few clothes as possible, but invest in outfits which proffer infinite variety. Separates and layers provide the answer, and fortunately this fashion seems to be everlastingly popular. Choose a basic colour – dark ones are most practical and give most scope –

and build around that. Today you can wear almost anything anywhere. Scarves, belts and junk jewellery can dress up the plainest basics, adapting them to suit the most formal and elaborate occasions.

Men are not quite so lucky, and in many households business suits are likely to knock quite a hole in the clothing budget, although the credit accounts operated by many stores are helpful in spreading the cost. Most men welcome the opportunity to get into more casual gear at home, however, and this habit as well as a little care and attention will preserve the active life of suits for a surprisingly long time, though it is essential to have a minimum of two if a suit is required for business wear.

A big problem is clothing for children. They seem to grow like mushrooms in the night, usually just after you have bought the most expensive item of their wardrobe. It goes without saying that one buys the largest size feasible, but style can help a lot – loose boxy lines with dropped shoulders will last for ages – children tend to grow up rather than out. School uniforms can be a real headache, and many of them could be more practical, but they are useful in so far as they limit competition for the latest fashion, and many schools now have uniforms which can be bought in chain stores at competitive prices. Most youngsters do want to exploit their own tastes in leisure clothes, and two wardrobes are virtually unavoidable. Groups of mums are getting together more and more to organize swops and hand-down sales. Happily, the ubiquitous blue denim takes care of most leisure requirements and practically forms an alternative 'uniform'!

It is better to avoid expensive 'special occasion' clothes for children. Often they are worn only once or twice before they are outgrown. A pretty blouse or a new shirt and tie are much cheaper than a dress or suit, and could be worn with a new skirt or trousers which will later earn their keep in the everyday wardrobe. Coats are the heaviest expense, but every child today seems to wear a duffel coat or anorak. If a coat must be purchased, a washable, showerproof, polyester/cotton with a zip-in cosy lining is the answer, since it can be worn all the year round, rain or shine. Washability is the prime criterion in all clothing for children. Brightly coloured cheap cottons, particularly corduroys and T-shirts, are likely to shed dye in the wash. For some odd reason this is a problem much more likely to be encountered in children's clothing – perhaps because of the popularity of bright colours and also because of attempts to produce cheap articles in the anticipation that they will not have to last long. It is no economy to dye everything in a wash load an unwanted shade of pink, though, so beware.

Quality

What do you look for in clothing? Two things probably – wearing quality and cleaning or washing quality. Price is not necessarily an indication of either. Wearing quality will depend on the fabric and on how well the garment is put together. Man-made fibres seem to wear practically forever, but they do have some disadvantages. They tend to be less absorbent than natural fibres (wool, silk, linen and cotton) which means they may feel sticky and clammy, especially in hot weather. They are not so warm as wool (nothing is), and they possess the property of building up static electricity, which attracts dirt and causes cling or, in extreme cases, crackles and sparks! New weaves and finishes are helping to overcome these snags, and man-made fibres blend very happily with natural ones, giving the best of both worlds – the wonderful wearing and crease-resistant properties of man-mades together with the warmth of wool or absorbency of cotton.

Good finish is important and a reliable brand name is probably the safest guide. Examine seams and buttonholes and see that there is room to sit down in skirts and trousers, and enough fabric across the shoulders of dresses, blouses and jackets to let the wearer reach forward easily. This is especially important for children.

Look for articles which can be washed. It will save you a fortune in dry cleaning bills, particularly if you are fond of light colours. White does not dry clean very successfully. Buy nothing unless it carries a care label, otherwise you will have no idea whether – or how – to wash or dry clean it, and mistakes are expensive. Never take a shop assistant's word for it if there is no label. With the best will in the world, she could be wrong!

Underpinnings

Underwear is worn for a number of reasons – warmth, hygiene and support. It has to take hard wear and frequent laundering so poor quality is a bad buy. Here it *is* an economy to have rather more than you need – it does not go out of fashion to any extent, and good rotation spreads wear.

Underwear is not much on view in the normal course of

things, so it is worth patching and darning to save money for more obvious attractions. Nylon, which becomes a dreary colour long before it wears out, can be dyed (see p. 95). You can do interesting things with tights by cutting off laddered legs and wearing two one-legged pairs but it seems simpler to wear laddered tights under slacks. Stockings are more economical. Thirty denier and fancy knits last longer and are warmer too. Buy 'indestructible' socks – they are, almost. They may wear out the feet but that is another matter! Some men insist on wool, which wears out more quickly, but most woollen socks are nylon reinforced, and it is possible to get nylon socks with wool inside. Hand knitted socks can be re-footed and, for this reason alone, socks are worth knitting if woollen ones are required. They are small enough to carry around and pick up in an odd moment, and, except for the heel and toe, there is no complicated pattern to follow.

Nappies

Nappies, are, of course, essential for babies and an extra half dozen can be one of the most useful gifts of all. Buy good quality – 'seconds' offer tremendous value. Nappies have to stand up to a lot of wear and tear, and have endless uses after the baby has no further need of them (see p. 125). For this reason stick to the traditional terry squares, as the shaped nappies have positively no other possibilities. Cotton towelling and muslin squares are easiest to keep white and fresh, and are also the most absorbent. Disposable nappies are very expensive, though useful in emergencies and when travelling.

What about sales?

Except for dedicated followers of fashion, I cannot imagine why people buy clothes at any other time. A plan of campaign is required, however, and you must have a clear idea of your *needs*. Don't get carried away with things which 'might come in useful'. If it is not something which you need *now*, no matter what the reduction in price, it is not a bargain. Always check whether sale goods are genuine stock reduced, 'special buys' or 'seconds'. The last two should be carefully examined.

Some sale goods are damaged – there may be a button missing or some bad stitching. Investigate carefully and consider whether you can replace and repair easily. If articles are stained or soiled they will have to be washed or dry cleaned before they can be worn. Some stains are easy to remove and general grubbiness will wash out, but it is something of a risk if stains are conspicuous and severe. 'Seconds' usually have minor faults, and represent particularly good value in underwear, socks, tights, knitwear, shirts and shoes.

'Nearly New' shops can be a source of wonderful buys, sometimes things may have been worn only once, sometimes not at all. Organize 'Exchange and Mart' sessions with friends and patronize the local jumble sales. Get there early! Garments which are unattractive in themselves often have great potential for re-making into children's outfits.

Make it yourself

If you can sew and knit – you've got it made. If you can't – learn. It is more than worth the effort. During the war years the only way to acquire a wardrobe was to make it – and make it out of cast-offs into the bargain. Necessity is a great teacher, and having to unpick something first does give one a much better understanding of how it goes together. I remember being astonished to see what a sleeve looked like laid out flat!

Buy a simple pattern and try making something out of an old garment or jumble sale buy first – you have nothing to lose! Don't attempt a garment for a very small child – this can be difficult to handle for a beginner. Beware of friends who offer assistance and then do it all for you – that doesn't help *you* when your friend is not around. Skirts, nighties, sleeveless tunics and pinafores are good starters. You only need to produce one snappy wearable article and you're away!

Sewing machines

But how, you may ask, do I put the proposed garment together? What about buying a sewing machine? Perhaps you could borrow one until your enthusiasm is established. A sewing machine in regular use is an investment which pays back the initial outlay over and over. There is absolutely no need for a very expensive model which does everything. (I got rid of mine, preferring the simple model!) A machine which will stitch two pieces of fabric together rather faster and firmer than your own nimble or not-so-nimble fingers is all that is required. A good reconditioned model can be bought very reasonably and you can always trade it in for something more versatile if and when your skill and finances improve, but most people find a simple model is all they need. Attachments for buttonholing and hemming can be added and my own experience suggests that the older second-hand models are often more reliable in all respects. A sewing machine is invaluable for repair jobs, too, as it gives a stronger result than hand sewing.

Knitting

There are quite definitely two groups of people here – those who knit and those who don't. Frequently the knitters say they can't sew. This always defeats me, since they *have* to sew the flat pieces together to make a jumper or what have you!

Results are the great incentive. Easy styles, chunky wool and thick needles, should encourage anyone to have a try and it gets easier as you go on. Just in passing, men are credited with the invention of knitting, so anyone can do it! You can watch television at the same time, provided the pattern is not complicated, and thus make satisfying use of time which you might otherwise feel guilty about 'wasting'. Knitting can be a very soothing form of therapy – the resultant garment may even seem like a bonus!

Knitting machines

How many of these are lying abandoned in cupboards after an impulse buy? It takes time to learn to use a knitting machine, but once the techniques have been mastered, it can save money especially in families where there are several children. The stocking stitch jumpers and cardigans which are usually a feature of school uniform can be produced quickly and economically, but of course you still have to sew them up! Knitting machines will not be popular in the family living room, as they are noisy and will certainly interfere with reading, homework and television viewing. Knitting must be done either when the operator is alone, or the machine must be set up in another room.

Re-using wool

Jumpers can be unravelled and knitted up again in a smaller size or with short sleeves instead of long – there will be less yarn as you are bound to waste a little in the unpicking. As you unravel, wind the wool round a small tray or stiff card about 30 cm (1 ft) wide. Tie into a hank at about three points, remove from the card and wash carefully. The crinkles will then be removed to a large extent, and the wool can be rewound and used again. Stretching while drying will improve the effect even more, but the wool will then have a tendency to relax, and therefore shrink, the first time the new article is washed. Man-made fibres are less satisfactory for this purpose, but it still is worth a try.

Care of clothes
Clothes do respond to tender loving care. Cleaning is important (see pp. 110-14), but storage plays no less an important part in keeping things smart for as long as possible.

Most garments benefit from being stored on hangers if space will permit. Air and brush outdoor clothes and non-washables after every wearing – it is surprising how much dirt accumulates on the surface, especially in a city. Have things washed or cleaned before they get too dirty – soiling causes wear and so does the extra friction required to remove it.

Winter clothes should be clean when stored away for the summer and should be protected from moths by using polythene bags. Real fur is particularly vulnerable, so keep an eye on it and give it an occasional airing in the sunshine – this will discourage 'squatters'. Not everyone has mink, but sheepskin and rabbit are just as tasty to moth grubs.

The protection of clothing is a point worth mentioning. Wearing an apron, smock or overall, especially over non-washable garments, can save many a dry cleaning bill. Table napkins might be considered for this reason also – cotton seersucker could not be easier to wash and needs no ironing. Paper napkins are costly, and washable fabric ones will repay their initial cost very quickly indeed. The use of napkins will save many conspicuous food stains on garments.

Shoes
Shoes are worn for the protection and support of the feet, though some fashions would lead one to query this. From the health point of view, we would do much better to run around barefoot. This practice would also be a considerable saving as shoes are becoming more and more expensive. Most of us have worn shoes for so long that it would be uncomfortable to change our ways now, so it is hardly a practical proposition.

Buying shoes
The main consideration in the buying of shoes is comfort. We frequently sacrifice comfort for a particular colour, style or fashion. This can have a serious effect on the health and conformation of the feet, and also on the budget, because you

cannot wear uncomfortable shoes, so the money has been wasted. Feet should be properly measured and there should be plenty of room for the toes to spread normally, foot health depends on this. Slip-on shoes do not permit this spread, since the shoe is held on by compression between the toe and heel. A good shoe has some means of preventing the foot from sliding forward and compressing the toes, hence lacing, bar and ankle strap shoes are good.

It does not pay to be too economical. Generally speaking, you get what you pay for. With the wide variety of shoes available you can usually find the sort of shoe you want at several prices. A cheaper shoe may appear to give good value, but is unlikely to wear as well as a more expensive one. The other thing worth paying for is comfort: dearer shoes usually offer a better range of fittings, and a shoe which fits properly is likely to wear better. It is false economy to try and survive with one pair of shoes only – you need to alternate wear. Shoes, like people, are the better for regular rests. High fashion can be expensive both in terms of price and the lack of occasions to wear it. Choose 'go-anywhere' styles in hard-wearing finishes and remember you need one pair which is reasonably water-proof – the only *really* waterproof footwear is a pair of welling-ton boots or galoshes. Fashion boots are – fashion boots! Don't expect to wade through puddles or snow without getting wet feet, and possibly damaging the boots for good.

Quality

This is difficult to judge. Look at stitching, seams, and feel the inside finishes. Price and well-known brand names are good guides. Leather shoes are usually more expensive and may be smooth, grained, patent or suede. Synthetic 'leathers' are widely used and perfectly satisfactory, certainly as far as soles are concerned. Leather uppers permit water vapour to pass through and will stretch in wear. 'Poromerics', or synthetics, allow air to pass through, but recover their original shape when removed, so they *must* be a comfortable fit in the shop, as they will not stretch or 'wear in'. Plastic-coated fabric is cheapest as a rule and is found mainly in low-price fashion shoes.

Children's shoes

It is vitally important that children's shoes are properly fitted, as their feet are not fully formed and therefore very vul-nerable to damage by badly fitting shoes. Growing feet should be measured by an expert fitter every time new shoes are bought. Never buy shoes for a child without the child being there to try them on. To allow the feet to grow, the shoe should be about 1.5 cm ($\frac{5}{8}$ in) longer than the longest toe, but should not be so big that the foot slips from side to side. The shoe should fit firmly round the ankle. 'Sunday best' shoes are often a waste of money – they can be outgrown in six months. But the toes can be cut out of sandals, if they are only slightly too small.

It is unwise to hand shoes down from one child to another for the obvious reason that they will have worn into the shape of the original owner's feet and will be totally out of balance for anyone else.

Care of shoes

Wear new shoes for the first time on a dry day so that a coating of dirt and small stones can build up on the sole to increase water resistance.

Do not attach 'stick-on' soles without first enquiring in the shop – they can upset the balance of the shoe, and the retailer may refuse to accept complaints. Clean shoes regularly with the proper type of cleaner – ask about this when you buy the shoes. Smooth leather responds to a good wax polish which will preserve it and protect the surface. With synthetic, patent and plastic-coated shoes, wipe with a damp rag and follow manufacturer's instructions for polishing. Suede needs regular brushing and occasional treatment with a special suede cleaner. It is difficult to keep suede looking really smart and spotless and a special dirt-resistant spray can be used before shoes are first worn. Darker colours are a more practical buy. Greasy marks on light suede can be removed by brushing with fuller's earth or talcum. Dark colours need special grease remover.

Keep shoes aired after each wearing and store on shoe trees or stuff with newspaper. If they get wet, do not dry them in front of the fire. Place in a well-ventilated area with newspaper inside if they are really soaking. Never scrape mud off with a knife; use something less lethal. Have shoes repaired before the heels wear down badly; this will lengthen their life. If covered plastic heels are damaged, touch up the marks with matching enamel – you can buy it in tiny tins. Shoe colour can be changed with special paint, and it is very successful. This is useful when you simply must have shoes to match a particular outfit. This treatment will renew the appearance of an old pair – provided they are in good repair. You can also paint a bag to match.

Shoes which have become shabby before they are outworn can be repaired in other ways. Leather which has become dry and hard can be softened with saddle soap. Suede which is smooth in patches can be roughened again by holding in steam or rubbing gently with fine sandpaper. Alternatively, make suede shoes shiny by treating with wax shoe polish in the same shade or slightly darker. Hard rubbing and several applications will be required. Do not cast out shoes until all these possibilities have been explored.

Valeting

This rather quaint-sounding title encompasses all the things which would normally be done by a valet in the care of clothes – and a few other things as well. The storage (p.107) and laundering (chapter 6) of clothes have been dealt with, but dry cleaning, both home and commercial, must be considered also in terms of economy.

Clothes collect a formidable amount of dirt and soiling in daily wear. This is obvious on shirts, blouses and light coloured fabrics, but one sometimes overlooks the fact that the dark coloured heavy fabrics used in coats and suits collect even more, and they don't go in the tub weekly. Illustrations in dry cleaner's magazines sometimes show the amount of dirt which can accumulate in a suit after a month or two's wear. It is little wonder that articles seem lighter and thinner after this is removed! Dry cleaning is expensive, but do not economize too much. Articles which get over-soiled may have to go through the process more than once. This causes extra wear, as does the damage caused by soiling left in the fibres for a long time. Body acids, perspiration and atmospheric fumes all have this damaging effect. Cut down on cleaning by brushing garments regularly, and treating collars, cuffs and greasy marks with a solvent cleaner (p. 88). It is surprising how much dirt you can lift off in this way. Do not rub too hard or you will push the dirt in instead of taking it out. Treat stains immediately, before they set in (see chapter 7).

Sponging

If you want to revive the appearance of a jacket, skirt or trousers by pressing, brush or sponge first – failure to do this will mean that you are pressing surface dirt into the fabric. Never expect this to take the place of thorough dry cleaning.

For sponging, use a liquid detergent solution and avoid wetting the article too much. Rinse off with a cloth wrung out in clean water. Allow articles to dry off before pressing.

Pressing

The pressing action is different from the push and glide technique of ironing. The iron should be placed fair and square on damp muslin laid over the article, then lifted. Be sure the heat is suitable for the fabric below the muslin. Pressing dark fabrics with a steam iron only may lead to shine and glazing – it is better always to use muslin or a damp cloth.

Trousers

Press each leg separately and set the creases on their original line – 'tram lines' look worse than no crease at all.

Woollen skirts with baggy seats (and also baggy knees on trousers)

Lay flat on ironing board and gather baggy area together, as near as possible to the size it ought to be. Place a *very* damp cloth over this and use a pressing movement, but do not allow the weight of the iron to rest on the cloth. It will hiss merrily but this is exactly what you want. The steam will shrink the bagginess.

Note: This will NOT WORK WITH ACRYLICS – in point of fact it may have the opposite effect, so be sure the fabric is woollen.

Creases and pleats

They can be sharpened in several ways.

1 By rubbing with a dry bar of kitchen soap on the wrong side before pressing.

2 By using plastic stiffener sponged on wrong side.

3 By using proprietary aerosol or spray starch on the wrong side.

Shine

This is virtually impossible to remove from man-made fibres, but woollen materials, like the serge used for uniforms and school blazers, can be sponged with a solution of ammonia – 1 teaspoon to $\frac{1}{2}$ litre (1 pint) water. Rinse with a cloth wrung out in clean water and press in the usual way.

Commercial dry cleaning

This is not dry at all, as you may have observed for yourself at your local cleaners. Articles are tumbled in a machine with spirit cleaner which may contain a special detergent and even some water. You pay for the professionalism involved in the initial stain removal, and in the selection of the correct balance of cleaning solution. Some cleaners are undoubtedly better than others – shop around, and choose one who is a member of the Association of British Launderers and Cleaners. Their code of practice helps to safeguard you if things go wrong. Remove large expensive buttons from women's coats and suits – men's are usually standard and easy to replace. It could cost more to replace a whole set of buttons, should one get lost in the cleaning, than it does to clean the garment, so it *is* worth the bother.

Dry cleaning is a source of many complaints so do make a point of checking at the counter that the article is suitable for cleaning. Point out any special instructions and indicate stains which you have, or have not, treated – with all relevant information. When jersey articles are cleaned it is a very good idea to give the measurements. You may find it well worth while to write all this down and give a copy to the cleaner with a brief description of the article and your name. It only takes minutes and can help the cleaner as well as settling later arguments should they arise.

Coin-op cleaning
A useful way of cleaning everyday wear. It will not be as efficient or effective as the real professional job, and you have to do your own pressing. To get the best results, do not allow articles to get too dirty before cleaning. Treat stains if there is a steam gun for this purpose. Check garment labels for the circle with A, P or F in it. Should the letter be F, the article must be treated professionally. A and P are usually safe in a coin-op, but enquire if you are doubtful. Have enough articles to make up a load to get your money's worth. You could share a load with a friend.
Note: Air articles thoroughly before travelling in a car or bus with them. You could nod off in the car due to the fumes. It is not quite so serious on a bus but fumes could be unpleasant for the other passengers.

To clean hats
Felt hats can easily be cleaned at home and the results are very good. Hats are an expensive item and collect a lot of grime if worn regularly. Men's hats especially take quite a beating, as often the same one is worn daily. You need about ½ kg (1 lb) of either bran (available at health food store or pet shop) or resin-free sawdust. The first you would have to buy, the second can

be obtained from a joiner or carpenter, NOT from the local sawmill – as the sawdust *must* be resin-free, i.e. it must come from hard wood.

Take off the hat band and clean it and the inside band with spirit cleaner. You can also wash the ribbon or renew it, if you see fit. Pad a bowl of suitable size and place the hat over this, standing the lot on a large sheet of paper or polythene. Heat the bran or sawdust scattered on a tin in the oven until 'stinging hot' to touch. Rub the hot material all over the felt. The heat will melt the greasy soiling which is then absorbed by the bran or sawdust. Allow to cool, then brush off very thoroughly. Hold the hat in front of a steaming kettle, and reshape if necessary. Replace band.

To clean fur

Small pieces of real fur – collars, hats and gloves can be cleaned as above, but the bran or sawdust should not be so hot as the fur could be damaged. Silver sand (obtainable at hardware stores) should be used in the same way for long-haired fur, as bran or sawdust can be difficult to remove. Never wash real fur, and dry it carefully if it gets wet. Hang in a warm airy place, not in front of a fire.

White sheepskin lining can become very grubby looking and can be cleaned either by rubbing with warm plain flour (not all that economical) or by sponging with liquid detergent. Man-made furs can be treated this way also, though many of them are in fact fully washable.

Suede and leather garments

These must be professionally cleaned. As the garments cost a lot initially, it is worth it. Greasy stains can be treated with warm fuller's earth. Spirit cleaners are risky, as they can affect dye and leave a mark.

Some leather garments like skirts, gloves and shorts are washable, and will be labelled accordingly. Hand wash as wool and roll in an old towel or cloth before placing in the spin drier or passing through the wringer at a very low tension. Dry in a warm (not hot) atmosphere and rub articles occasionally while drying to keep the leather soft. Non-washable leather gloves, smooth leather coats and natural hide handbags can be cleaned with special leather soap which is obtainable in luggage departments, saddlers or ironmongers. Coloured leather handbags should *not* be polished with coloured shoe cleaner. It may rub off on clothing, especially on a wet day. Use neutral cleaner or a suitable furniture cream.

Suede bags and gloves are more difficult to maintain. Shine can be removed with fine emery paper or a rubber suede brush. Special suede cleaning products are available and are good value for money, but it is important that things should not be allowed to become too heavily soiled before these are used. Fuller's earth is effective in removing greasy stains – if they are very severe, treat with a paste of fuller's earth and a solvent cleaner (p. 88). Allow this to dry, then brush off gently. Test the effect of solvent cleaner before using on coloured suede.

Plastic

Plastic gloves and handbags should be sponged with a warm soapy solution, rinsed and rubbed up when dry. A soft brush can be used if necessary on plastic which has a grained finish. Polish should not be used on plastic as it will remain in a sticky layer on the surface. An exception to this is a colourless shoe cleaner recommended for plastic shoes. Biro stains on plastic are in the nature of a disaster, as they are virtually impossible to remove.

Many of the foregoing treatments are old-fashioned, but very well worth keeping in mind. Professional cleaning is expensive, and attention of the 'little and often' variety at home will keep garments looking fresh and smart between visits to the dry cleaners. Many cleaners provide a repair service. It is not cheap, but if an expensive garment has been torn or damaged you might be well-advised to have it professionally repaired. This does rather depend on your own skill with a needle, but a really invisible mend is difficult to accomplish.

chapter 10

REPAIRS AND MENDING

Mending is not nearly so much fun as making something new, and it is – or was – a disappearing art. Clothes were relatively inexpensive until quite recently, and it was so much easier to go and buy something new than to do a tedious mending job. Now, because of spiralling costs, there is not so much choice and we are learning to mend again. Modern techniques do make the task easier, but the stitch-in-time habit makes it easier still. It is cheaper and quicker to sew on one button than to buy a whole new set; a small hole soon becomes a big one; and it is much simpler to darn a thin place than a hole. Poor mending looks awful. Careful, neat repairs have a different air about them, and it is worth persevering to acquire reasonable skill with a needle.

Patches

Patching should be done with matching fabric where possible. If it isn't possible, consider making a feature of the patch. Hosts of bright patches are available in the shops. On children's clothes and casual wear patches are attractive and acceptable; less so on business wear or your best sheets! Sometimes a patching piece can be obtained from a hem, seam or facing – this means you have to replace it too, of course, with a non-matching piece. The patch should be big enough to cover the hole and any worn part surrounding it, otherwise it will soon break loose from its moorings. The type of patch and the means of attaching will depend on the fabric.

1. *Print patch:* is usually put on the right side for the obvious reason that it is easier to match the pattern that way. Cut a square or oblong piece to cover the hole and worn area, matching the pattern. Leave enough for 12 mm ($\frac{1}{2}$ in) turnings. Turn in a single fold and tack all round (1a). Now place patch in position over the hole, matching pattern on right side of garment (1b). Tack and stitch in position (1c). Hand hemming is neater but machining may be stronger.

Turn to wrong side and trim worn part away to within 12 mm ($\frac{1}{2}$ in) of the stitching. This should coincide with the turnings of the patch. Blanket stitch the two raw edges together (1d). Do not catch in the actual patching piece. This is not the strongest type of patch, since there is only one row of stitching holding it on, but it is the most invisible.

2. *Plain patch:* this is a stronger patch and may be hand or machine stitched. It is usually placed on the wrong side of the article being repaired. Cut patch as for 1. Turn in single fold on to *right* side of patch (2a). Apply patch to wrong side of article, tack and stitch (2b).

Turn to right side and trim away worn part to 15 mm ($\frac{5}{8}$ in) from the stitching. Make a tiny snip into each corner so that the edge can be turned in neatly 12 mm ($\frac{1}{2}$ in) (2c). Tack and stitch (2d).

3. *Stretch patch:* with the many knitted and stretch fabrics on the market, a different technique must be used since this type of patch will have to stretch with the garment. In days gone by this was known as a 'flannel' patch, and applied with herring-bone stitch (shown in 3b). If your machine does a suitable stitch, i.e. zigzag, this could be used, but ordinary machining is too rigid.

The procedure is the same as for the plain patch, but *no* turnings are used.

Iron-on patches
If the thought of sewing at all is positively abhorrent, consider an iron-on patch. This is useful for jeans, casual wear and children's clothes.

There is also an iron-on 'bonding' material (similar to iron-on interfacing), and though it is really meant as an easy way of joining two surfaces without sewing (e.g. – a hem) it can be used for repairs and means that you make your own iron-on patch with similar fabric if it is available.

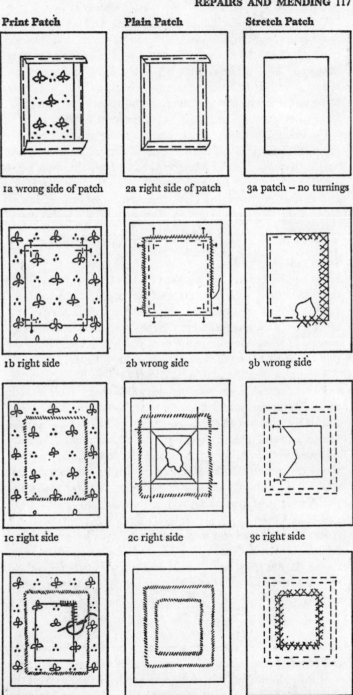

Print Patch

Plain Patch

Stretch Patch

1a wrong side of patch

2a right side of patch

3a patch – no turnings

1b right side

2b wrong side

3b wrong side

1c right side

2c right side

3c right side

1d wrong side finished

2d right side finished

3d right side finished

Choose an iron-on fabric suitable for, and as similar as possible in weight to, the fabric you want to patch. A fine fabric patched with thick material will be clumsy and have a 'dragged' look, while too fine a patch will be ineffective on heavy fabric. It will not be strong enough to hold, and may come off. It is wise to catch the edges of tears or holes together with fishbone stitch (shown in 5a) to prevent fraying.

Use matching thread. Apply patch according to instructions supplied. Press firmly with an iron set at a suitable temperature for the *fabric being patched*. (Check when you buy that your iron-on does not require too high a temperature – nylon, acrylics and rayons might melt.) Cool, and test for adhesion. If unsatisfactory, repeat the process. Properly applied, the patch will withstand washing and dry cleaning.

Shirt collars

Shirts can sometimes be purchased with an extra collar. Wash this occasionally with the shirt, so that it does not look too new. Instructions for changing the collar are given with it. With any other type of shirt, see whether the collar can be turned. If there are little pockets for collar stiffeners, you will not be able to do this – a point to watch next time you buy a shirt.

Unpick the neckband and remove the collar. Strengthen the worn part with iron-on bonding, described above. Now replace the collar in the reversed position, tack and machine stitch. Finish the ends very firmly. You will now have to sew up the buttonhole and make a new one at the opposite side. (Take the measurements from the sewn-up one.) Replace the button over the sewn-up buttonhole. A new collar can be cut from the tail of the shirt, using the old one as a pattern, but you need some skill for this. An interfacing will be necessary.

Note: Much of the wear is caused by scrubbing before washing. Soak a very soiled shirt instead, and rub soap in the dirty crease. If you must scrub, do it gently from the wrong side to push the dirt back out. Scrubbing on the right side only pushes dirt in.

Cuffs

As with the collar, these can sometimes be turned, but double cuffs are not now common. A single cuff can simply be reduced in width. Slit the fold where the frayed edge is and trim off the worn part. Reduce the interfacing by 6 mm ($\frac{1}{4}$ in) and fold the two cuff edges inwards to cover it. Be careful to get all the raw edges enclosed at the corners. Machine stitch along the edge. If you have no machine, make a slightly deeper turning on the inner edge, and hem by hand so that it is not seen from the right side. Iron-on bonding could be used for this repair too – especially if the fraying is on the inside. Insert a strip of the iron-on fabric and press the frayed cuff fabric over it.

Note: A common cause of cuff wear is a watch strap. Spread the wear by alternating the wrist from time to time.

Leather patches

These are obtainable for patching or strengthening elbows of tweed sports jackets. They are hand stitched in position and a suitable leather needle and thread should be used. The stitching must not be too tight or it will tear the leather when the elbow is flexed. Strengthening bands may be stitched round the cuffs also, and this could add some useful length to a sleeve. A strip of fine leather stitched inside the trouser leg where it rubs against the shoe will prolong the life of worsted and woollen trousers. Trousers containing man-made fibre are less prone to fraying.

Darns

Darning is mainly used to repair holes and worn, thin parts of knitted fabrics and to strengthen weakened fibres in household linen and clothing. Done in good time, darning can lengthen the life of a garment by months, especially if it is done as soon as a thin place appears. Darns are successful on such materials as knitted fabrics, jersey, wool, flannel, tweed, net, woven cotton and polyesters. Darn on the wrong side, wherever possible, using matching yarn. You might daringly use a contrast if you are confident that the result will be very neat, but the thickness of the yarn must be as similar as possible. Darn beyond the worn part and leave tiny loops to allow for shrinkage of wool. If you pull the threads too tightly the darn will pucker the surrounding fabric. Darns should not have straight edges – irregularities help to distribute the strain. A last useful reminder is to work the second set of stitches – the 'weaving' ones – diagonally. This is done on knitted fabrics to allow stretch. Small tears on woven fabrics are more easily darned than patched and the technique is the same. The diagrams on p. 120 show how to darn a hole, tear or slit.

To darn a hole

4a Weave needle in and out to make an irregular diamond shape and work beyond the worn area surrounding the hole

4b Turn darn round and weave across hole in opposite direction leaving small loops at each end of line of stitching

4c When darning a knitted fabric make sure you catch in any stitches in the fabric that are likely to run. Follow 4a but on turning darn round, weave the second set of stitches diagonally across the first set of stitches

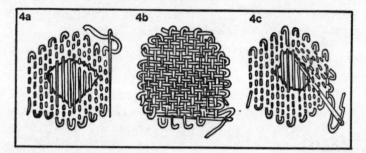

To darn a tear

5a Fix a piece of paper behind tear to hold the edges in position and fishbone stitch (shown below) edges of tear together. Use fine thread

5b Darn across base well beyond tear

5c Turn work round and darn across other part of tear, forming a solid square at the corner. Remove paper

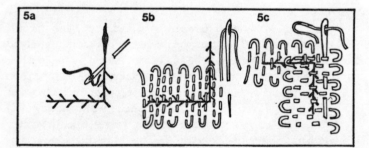

To darn a slit

6 Darn in rows across slit keeping the edges of the darn parallel to slit. Darn across slit in opposite direction, again keeping edge of darn parallel to slit

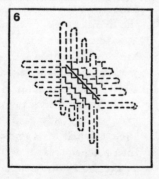

Strengthening

This is the stitch in time. Strengthening can be done the easy way by using iron-on materials and it is a good idea to keep an emergency kit of this kind. Frayed edges, small cuts and rips and dropping hems are quickly put right and this is a great way out for non-sewers. It is certainly quicker even for sewers, but repairs in critical areas are better entrusted to a strong stitching job. Some iron-on repair materials are much better than others, and as it is such a constantly changing market, you must try shopping around and experimenting to discover the best. None will be any use unless you follow the instructions to the letter.

Tape

Ordinary white tape stitched to frayed or worn edges of towels and sheets will prolong their useful life considerably. Or you could simply trim the worn edge and turn in a hem, if you can afford to lose the width.

Tape is also useful for repairing buttonholes, especially on pyjamas which are the most likely garments to suffer this sort of damage. If the buttons are also torn out by the roots, a strip of tape machined between facing and garment will give them a strong hold again.

To repair a torn buttonhole

7 To strengthen and repair the outer edges of buttonholes, stitch a length of tape along the edge on the inside of the garment. Re-do buttonholing over the new material

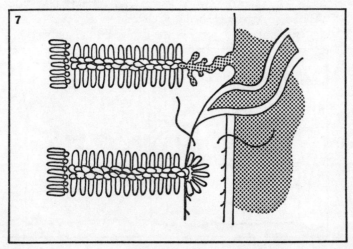

7

Swiss darn

When heels and elbows of hand knitted garments wear thin, a Swiss darn will give a much neater result than the kind of darn which is used over a hole. The secret is to follow the loops of the original knitting as shown in diagram 8.

Swiss darn

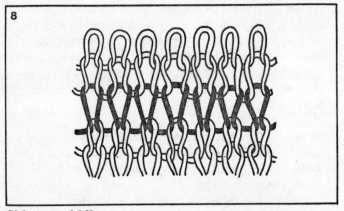

Sides to middle

When sheets wear in the middle, cut them in half down the centre, and join the selvedges. There are several ways of doing this, but the main aim is to achieve a really flat join, since the sleeper will be lying on it. If the selvedges are not worn, lay one on top of the other, overlapping about 6 mm ($\frac{1}{4}$ in) and do a double row of machine stitching (9a), or zigzag stitch if your machine has such finesse. The edges could also be oversewn by hand. This gives the neatest join of all, but it does take time. If the outside edges have hems, these must be unpicked or cut off, and a flat seam used to join the two edges (9b and 9c).

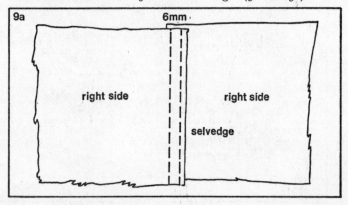

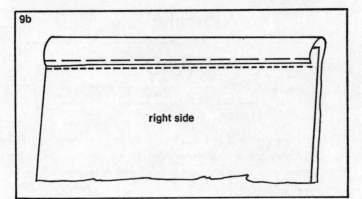

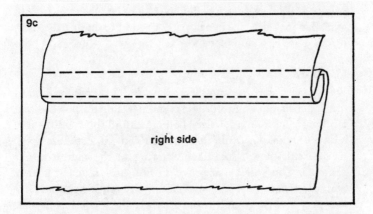

New hems will be required at the sides and also where the new join comes at top and bottom. It is best to do this repair before the sheets get too worn in the middle, otherwise you may have to cut off quite a large area, thus making the sheet much narrower. There is little wear on the tuck-in sides, but don't wait until there is going to be nothing left to tuck in!

A blanket can be treated in exactly the same way, but a single seam should be made and pressed open. The raw edges should be herringbone stitched by hand or zigzag stitched on a machine.

chapter 11

ODDS AND ENDS
AROUND THE HOUSE

This is a chapter full of miscellaneous hints. If some of them seem familiar it is because they keep on being 'discovered' by succeeding generations as economic need demands, whilst in periods of affluence they fade away again but never quite die – like the old soldiers they are. There are also snippets from newspapers and magazines which you may have meant to cut out and keep for reference but never got round to finding the time, the scissors, or a safe place for keeping!

Use it up

Empty every sort of container *completely*. This goes for food in tins, packets, jars and bottles; cosmetics, talcum powder and toothpaste, cleaning powders, detergents and shoe polish – and a lot more besides. Drain them, rinse them out, cut them open, scrape with plastic spatulas according to the nature of the contents. You will be surprised to find how much you have been throwing away. This may not save much in one sense, but you may as well get full value for the money you have spent. Value for money is the basis of sensible modern living.

Fabric and household linen

Never throw out any fabric. Certainly, you will have to find somewhere to store the bits and pieces, but two days after you throw or give something away – you want it. (That is somebody's law!) In more affluent times it may not have mattered so much. Now it is worth the trouble of making storage space. Dressmaking scraps may later be required for repairs, and they are also useful for patchwork of a more decorative kind. Bigger pieces might make aprons, sun-tops, head squares, scarves, cushion covers or a child's garment. Leftover curtain fabric will recover cushions, make chairbacks or coverings for storage boxes. Pieces too small to interest you, will keep a small child happily amused for hours.

Old clothes, as suggested in chapter 9, can be made into something else if the fabric is in good condition. Unpick (you can cut if you haven't the patience to unpick, but it does waste fabric unnecessarily) and launder the garments – they take up less room stored flat if you want to use them at a later date. Keep all buttons, zips and trimmings – they cost almost as much as the fabric for a new garment. Consider the possibilities of the real 'rags'. Old woollen rags are worth money – so sell the last shreds! Old cotton and woollen undergarments make excellent dusters and polishing cloths. Surely no one *buys* dusters? There is not very much you can do with nylon, but old tights can be snipped up to make stuffing for soft toys or scatter cushions. Old woollen socks make good polishing cloths stuffed with other rags, while stretch nylon socks pulled *over* shoes give a good grip on icy pavements.

Household linen can stay with you till it drops to pieces. When mended beyond hope of further repair, sheets may still have good corners which would make under-pillowcases, cot sheets or tea towels – linen is especially good for this purpose and you can stitch two thicknesses together if the fabric is very thin. The very last bits could be finished off as dusters, bandages or nappy liners. Don't forget you may occasionally need a dust sheet. The possibilities of nylon and polyester and cotton are more limited. They probably never wear out, but become so grotty in their old age that their last useful function is likely to be that of a dust sheet. Blankets can be cut down for cots or used as underblankets. They make good padding for upholstered seats and tie-on cushions for dining chairs, and also for insides of oven gloves.

Towels wear thin in the middle, but the corners make good face cloths and dishcloths. The thin bits are fine for general household use. Keep old towels in the garage or garden shed for hand wiping. Last uses might be for car, tool or metal cleaning. If you have a dog you will need an old towel for him.

Nappies, if still in good condition, make useful child-size towels. Dye them attractive colours with cold water dyes to change their original character. It only takes a few minutes to add a name or initial in chain stitch. Cut in quarters, a nappy will give four good face cloths – blanket stitch or zigzag the edges. Worn nappies have uses similar to old towels.

Slimy face cloths and sponges are revolting objects. The problem is more likely to occur in hard water areas because of the scum which forms with soap. Prevention is better than cure. Wash face cloths weekly along with towels (Hot 60°C, 140°F wash code 2) in a non-soapy detergent. Rinse them thoroughly after use. Treat sponges the same way. Another method is to boil for ten minutes in vinegar and water: 1 tablespoon vinegar to $\frac{1}{2}$ litre (1 pint) water. Rinse in clear water with a few drops of ammonia.

Knitting wool
Keep enough for darning matching garments. Use up small pieces by knitting toys. Brightly coloured leftovers make knitted or crochet squares which can be joined up into cushion covers, pram covers or blankets, depending on your enthusiasm.

Wallpaper and vinyl
Useful for lining drawers and shelves or for covering school books distinctively. One roll might be enough to make a decorative panel, and if it is vinyl, it could be a splashback in kitchen or bathroom. Cover strong cardboard boxes for storing toys and games.

Lino and vinyl
Cuttings make a good surface for shelves, unit and table tops. This is quite simply applied with a suitable adhesive and is much cheaper than buying new laminated plastic.

Carpet
Leftovers should be kept for patching. A large piece can be bound and used as a rug. The best pieces of old carpets may be used in the same way. A patchwork carpet can be made from the best parts of old ones or from carpet samples. Use adhesive carpet tape to join them. All the pieces should be about the same thickness or it will be uneven to walk on. Old or leftover carpet felt is good for lagging pipes and providing insulation.

Paint
When you finish a painting job, seal the surface of the paint in the tin with foil before hammering on the lid. Paint will keep longer this way and the uses of leftover paint are legion.

Soap
Shred scraps of household and toilet soap and boil up with enough water to cover, until dissolved. The resulting jelly is useful for washing tights and underwear. It is better avoided in dishwashing if scented toilet soap has been used, otherwise it is handy for most other household purposes.

Packaging

If you object to paying the extra for modern packaging, at least
see that you put as much of it as you can to further good use.
Polythene bags, plastic wrappings, foil containers, tubs, cartons
and jars can all be re-used many times. Used paper bags do for
wrapping up rubbish, and cut open, the inside surfaces will
clean out greasy pans or drain fried food.

Fuel saving

Keeping warm is a basic necessity for all of us, and a large slice
of any budget goes in the payment of fuel bills. Fuel prices have
risen dramatically and we are as rapidly returning to the fuel-
saving practices of wartime – not because the power is not
available, but because we can no longer afford to pay for it in
thoughtless quantity. (See also p. 15).

Conserving heat

There is no point in getting hysterical over switching off a 60
watt light bulb, or wondering whether it is more economical
to whisk a sponge by hand than with an electric mixer. The
saving involved is minimal. *Heat* is the expensive item, and
every time you use fuel to produce heat it costs you money.

The first consideration, therefore, is to conserve heat. The
better insulated the home, the lower the consumption of fuel.
To ensure sizeable savings you need at least 75 mm (3 in) of
insulation. Insulate the loft (well worth the cost) and the walls
too, if you can afford to. Double glazing on the other hand, is
not considered by the experts to be worth its high cost. Draught
excluders and thick curtains or blinds have a similar effect at a
fraction of the cost. Draught excluders should be fitted on doors,
especially outside ones. The heat loss round an average door is
equivalent to that of a hole big enough to accommodate a
football. You would soon get that filled up! Letter boxes and
keyholes allow heat to escape also, so devise a method of
reducing this – a good spring on the flap, plastic foam around
it and a flap for the keyhole. Keep doors shut to prevent loss of
warmth. A spring closure on outside doors would repay its cost
very quickly, though it could take a toll in young fingers in a
family home.

If your home is well-insulated you will not need so much fuel
in the first place, but conserve it further by fitting room thermo-
stats if you have central heating. Edge temperatures down
gradually until people begin to complain of the cold! Time

clocks will control the use of heat – especially useful if you are out all day – and they can be purchased to fit on to individual electric appliances.

Water heating is particularly expensive if you use an immersion heater. Opinions vary about the most economical way to use these and no one seems to have found the complete answer. It depends on individual needs, but some points are helpful. If you are out all day, switch off. Switching on when you come home at night gives hot water for washing up and baths, and if you have a well-lagged tank you can switch off at bedtime if you prefer a morning bath, as the water will still be hot enough. But showers are much more economical than baths as less than half the amount of water is required. An immerser which has two elements for 'sink' and 'bath' is useful. An instantaneous, or sink, water heater is more economical for washing up and for supplying small quantities of water. There are no long runs of pipe in which several costly gallons of hot water will be wasted every time you run the hot tap. Use a washing up bowl instead of the sink for dish washing. The kettle is an economic way of heating water, particularly if it switches itself off when it reaches boiling point. Heat only as much water as you need. If you live alone, or have a penchant for frequent single cups of tea, a small immerser (available in large department stores) which clips into a cup is the best idea of all.

Cooking

Strictly speaking, it is not necessary to cook food, but a diet of raw meat, lettuce, carrot and switched eggs would have a very limited appeal. Cooking improves the appearance, flavour and digestibility of food and, as we are mostly accustomed to a cooked diet, the possibilities of significant savings in this area are few.

Pressure cookers do save fuel and they are a good buy, since several foods can be cooked at once if necessary. Double and triple pans which fit on one hotplate are also good but if you can't afford them, wrap vegetables and potatoes in foil, or boil-in-the-bag-plastic, and cook them in the stew – three for the price of one! There are many adaptations of this idea – investigate the possibilities. Make full use of the oven when it is on. You can cook vegetables and stew fruit in casseroles or pie dishes covered with foil. (Wash the foil and use it again and again!)

Lighting and electric motors

These are not major consumers of electricity, and it is not wise to have the family groping around with low wattage bulbs in every socket. It is not good for the eyesight and could be dangerous. The motors in appliances run for many hours on 1 unit of electricity and it is most unlikely that significant savings could be gained from banning their use. Concentrate all your efforts on conserving *heat*; remember it is the greedy one every time you switch on!

It is obvious from all this that you may very well have to spend in order to save, but the rising cost of fuel suggests that such investments are a very good hedge against inflation. Off-peak electricity may be worthy of consideration in some circumstances, but there are differing views about this, so make enquiries locally about tariff and installation costs. Find out from people who use it whether they think it is a big saving and also what are the good and bad features.

Gas and oil

Most of the foregoing points apply to gas and oil also. The big advantage of gas as fuel is flexibility of control – you can reduce heat instantly. Not everyone can have gas – the bottled variety is the only possibility for those not connected to a mains supply. Check at the local gas showroom that your home is operating on the correct tariff.

Solid fuel

Many solid fuel appliances are versatile. A well-insulated stove can heat water, heat the kitchen *and* do the cooking. Room heaters will normally heat water and/or several radiators. The look of a 'living fire' appeals to the primitive in most of us, and modern appliances do get the very best from costly fuel.

But if you have an open, yawning, old-fashioned grate, ready to gobble up coal by the bagful, sending much of the valuable heat up into the outside atmosphere, then reduce the size of the grate for a start by adding more firebricks. And always try to buy fuel during the summer when it is cheaper – if you don't have suitable storage space, investigate whether it would be possible to organize it. What you spend on a new (lockable) coal bunker could be paid back very quickly in summer savings. Those who live in smokeless zones are restricted in their choice of fuels, but in other areas wood-gathering expeditions provide free fuel. (You may need permission to remove fallen timber and you will certainly NOT be permitted to fell trees!) Fir cones are easy to gather in a basket and make good firelighters – or a decorative filling for an empty grate.

Coal dust and slack should be used up. It can be slightly dampened and placed directly on the fire, or shovelled into paper bags or sugar cartons and used like coal lumps.

Coal briquettes are made by mixing 1 part cement and 10 parts coal dust with enough water to make a stiff paste. Pack into flower pots or boxes and turn out when set. Only do this if you have either a vast amount of coal dust, or a small amount of cement to use up! It would not be worth buying a bag of cement.

Keep your chimney well-swept. Do it yourself if possible. Brushes can be hired, borrowed or purchased by a group. Clean chimneys give a better fire and prevent furnishings from being damaged by a smoky fire. A severe down-draught can be cured by fitting an H cowl, which will soon save its cost in redecorating expenses. Coal which has been dipped in a solution of washing soda and dried off is reputed to burn longer. It is more economical to build a really good fire which will burn for hours if you leave it *alone*. Heavy-handed work with the poker on three miserable lumps will give no value whatever.

Round the house

China and glass

Careful storage will extend the life of crockery. Hang cups on hooks and stack plates in reasonable piles. The one on the bottom has to take the strain of the whole pile – try lifting the pile and you will feel the extent of this strain! A plate stacker is a good buy. Glasses should not be stored upside down, or inside each other unless they are made for that purpose. Even with the best of care, glasses seem to have a short life in most homes. Stronger plastic or earthenware beakers could be used for everyday drinking.

Buy crockery in sales and never consider a tea or dinner set which cannot be bought piece by piece to replace breakages – enquire how long the pattern is likely to be available. Buy to suit your own life style – there is plenty of choice. Bone china is very expensive but amazingly strong. The cheaper types of china and porcelain are the most popular, and many of them are available in matching ovenware, which can be used as serving dishes. Toughened, patterned glass and the wide variety of modern pottery are also versatile and practical for

family use, though some are inclined to chip. Glazed earthenware is cheapest of all, but it too shares this unfortunate tendency to chip. Fit rubber tap protectors to cut down the hazards
of chipping and cracking. If you own a dishwasher buy dish-
washer-proof patterns.

Pots and pans

Look after these expensive items. Soak them after use and keep
the outsides clean – they heat more efficiently if you do. Never
put them away damp with the lids on – aluminium will 'pit',
especially in soft water. Do not use soda to clean aluminium
pans – they dissolve (though not immediately and spectacu-
larly). Staining in enamel pans can be removed by adding a
few drops of bleach to the panful of cold water. Rinse it well
afterwards. Non-stick surfaces need gentle treatment. When
the coating wears off it can be re-sprayed, but this has to be
carefully done. If your water is very hard keep a marble in the
kettle to prevent furring. Very soft water can corrode an
aluminium kettle, especially if it is left in a warm place with
water always in it. Few places in Britain have this problem!

Some inexpensive cleaners

Manufacturers are anxious to convince you of the wonders
their wares will perform. The wares are frequently composed
of very simple ingredients, many of which you may already
have in the house. Aerosols are a very expensive way of buying
products – you may consider it justified in some instances, but
you would do well to look for a tin, bottle or jar of similar
product. Try some of the old-fashioned methods which follow.

Glass, windows, pictures and mirrors A damp chamois leather,
special window cloth or damp newspaper is all you need to use
if the glass is not very dirty. Windows in city homes are likely
to collect more grime and heavy smokers cause nicotine staining on glass, so a more powerful cleaner will be needed. Try
one of these three.
1 1 tablespoon household ammonia in 2 litres ($\frac{1}{2}$ gal) water.
2 Methylated spirit.
3 A mixture of paraffin, methylated spirit and water in equal
quantities. Shake well together and use on a soft cloth. Allow
to dry, then polish up the glass.
Paintwork Add 1 tablespoon washing soda to liquid detergent
solution.

Wallpaper Clean by rubbing with stale bread or cleaning dough made with:

8 tablespoons flour and 4 tablespoons white spirit. Mix to a thick paste, adding a little warm water and kneading well. Use in long sweeping strokes, always keeping a clean surface towards the wallpaper. Remove greasy marks with a paste of fuller's earth and turps. Spread on and leave to dry.

Refrigerators, crockery, Thermos flasks Bicarbonate of soda is a good stain remover and deodorant. Use dry and rub on stains. For soaking a Thermos or washing out fridge or freezer, dissolve 2-3 teaspoons bicarbonate of soda in 1 litre (2 pints) warm water. (Bicarbonate of soda is also useful for removing fruit juice stains, soothing heatspots and sunburn, and as an emergency toothpaste.)

Drains Regular flushing with boiling hot washing soda solution will help to prevent grease clogging up the drains. Put a few lumps over the grid and pour boiling water through. If the drain does block, and you cannot lay hands on a suction cup, place a bucket below the U-bend and remove the screw. Clear the blockage with wire and flush with clean water – have a spare bucket handy, and don't empty the first bucket into the sink while the screw is still off the bend! After replacing the screw, flush with the boiling hot washing soda solution to get the waste pipe as clean as possible.

Note: Don't pour fat down the drain. Why are you wasting it anyway? Strain and use again!

Ovens This is 'hate job' number one! Make it a rule to wipe out the oven after use, while it is still warm. (You will probably never do it – but it *is* undoubtedly the quickest, cheapest, easiest way.)

An inexpensive method – provided things have not got really out of hand – is to place a small piece of cotton rag and 1-2 tablespoons ammonia in an old saucer. Stand this in the oven overnight, and wash out the oven next day with hot detergent suds and abrasive if necessary.

Another easy way is to soak removable sides, top and shelves in a boiling solution of washing soda. You need a big enough container of course, and a wash boiler or twin tub washing machine without a central agitator could be used. Be careful not to scratch surfaces.

Note: Do not carry out these procedures with special 'Stay-clean' oven linings. Always remember to check your instruction book.

Bathroom Use paste or liquid cleaners. Harsh abrasives scratch surfaces and make them more difficult to clean. Pastes are the most economical – not everyone realizes there are such things! Methylated spirit removes hair lacquer from mirrors. Add 1 tablespoon ammonia to 2 litres ($\frac{1}{2}$ gal) warm water for washing tiles. This can also be used for cleaning bath and basin. Bleach will clean and disinfect the lavatory but note that bleach must *never* be mixed with any other lavatory cleaner – toxic fumes may result. To get rid of unpleasant smells quickly and cheaply, strike one or two matches.

Personal hygiene Soap, shampoo, toothpaste and disinfectant are all necessary purchases. Save on them as much as possible. Get down to basics. Soap is for cleansing – fancy additives cost more and no one has yet proved that they do anything in particular, so stick to cheaper brands and large sizes. Store soap for some time before use – place it in drawers and cupboards with linen and underwear. It hardens, and will last much longer in use. Keep it on a drained surface, not sitting in a little puddle of water. Shampoos are also credited with miraculous powers, but are basically detergents. Protein, egg and olive oil sound interesting, but there is no evidence to support the fact that they even remain on the hair after rinsing. Spending the money on protein, egg and olive oil to be consumed as *food* is of much greater potential benefit to the hair! A make-up expert recently assured me that a certain liquid detergent makes an excellent shampoo, but if you don't feel inclined to experiment, look for good value in large size bottles, cheaper brands and special offers. Large containers of 'Family Talcum' are also a saving for everyday use. A good toothbrush is a top priority, and if it is properly used there is no real need for toothpaste at all. With the exception of those with fluoride, which you may consider a worthwhile additive, buy the cheapest toothpaste you can find. Hydrogen peroxide can be used on the skin quite safely. Bleach is a useful general disinfectant.

Maintenance

Neglect of the structure of your home can result in large repair bills. Carry out regular check-ups – small faults can be quickly and easily dealt with. Anticipate every kind of trouble – pessimists and economists have a great deal in common!

Pests

Keep the place clean, dry and well-ventilated. Leftover food should be under cover and your refuse should be in a firmly closed dustbin which is regularly disinfected. Bin liners are quite expensive and unnecessary. Paint the inside of the bin with anti-rust paint and line your bin with clean newspaper. Serious pest infestation may call for professional advice. Telephone the public health department.

Woodworm and dry rot are serious problems. Keep a watchful eye for any sign of woodworm in the wood in attics and other out-of-the-way places. You are very likely to spot badly infested furniture, which should be got rid of as soon as you do – but if the house structure is affected it is another matter. Quick treatment will save a major and expensive undertaking. The same applies to dry rot which lurks in dark, dank, unventilated places.

Painting and repairs

Everyone is aware that it is cheaper to do their own interior and exterior decoration, but don't cut corners and waste your time by buying cheap paint, or skimping on the number of coats. Do the job properly and take time to it. You *hate* painting? Change the colour scheme for a start – that makes the job more interesting. Putting white paint on white paint is too boring a proposition for the non-enthusiast. Think positively, while you toil, of all the money you are saving, and be glad you don't have to do this for a living. Don't perch on ancient rickety ladders. The consequences could be disastrous and expensive. If you have a lot of high-up work to do, hire the proper scaffolding. The money is well spent, and you will still be saving a great deal on a professional job. While you are in high places, clean out roof gutters and inspect flashings on chimneys. Look out for loose roof tiles, and cracks in roughcasting, brick and stonework. Small repairs to mortar are quite easily done. Woodwork round windows should be inspected for damp and rot and loose putty which needs replacing. All these are rather tedious fiddly jobs which get put off for any plausible reason. Get them out of the way before they become more serious problems – none is beyond the ability of an amateur. There is no shortage of suitable literature – and your local library will help. It is more than likely that friends or neighbours will have the necessary expertise – enlist their help and advice.

Tool kit

The more you are going to do it yourself, the more you will come to realize that you cannot really depend forever on a nail file and a penknife – even if it has the bit for taking things out of horses hoofs! Buy the best tools you can afford – you could budget for one a month – and keep them in a suitable box or bag to protect your investment and to have them to hand whenever required. Warning: tools cost a lot of money, never lend them lightly.

It is always useful to keep a large box of assorted treasure – nails, pins, tacks, screws, hooks, chalk, scissors, adhesives, twine, masking and insulating tape, etc. – beside the tool kit.

The table on p. 136 represents a handy tool kit, the items in bold type would make a basic tool kit for jobs around the house.

Trading skills

Calling out a tradesman to do a simple repair job like replacing a sash cord or a tap washer is a costly exercise. There are two alternatives. Learn how to do the job yourself or get someone else to do it for you. One cannot go on scrounging indefinitely, and some kind of repayment must be made – trade skills! This is already being done in some places with great success, and the idea originated in baby-sitting on a 'credit' rather than a financial reward system.

Most of us are good at, or reasonably keen on, some aspect of 'do-it-yourself' – necessity forces us. If your forte is home decorating, car maintenance or gardening, for example, you could trade these skills for dress- or curtain-making, joinery or electrical work. It can be done quite informally among a circle of good friends, but, like group purchase, it is better when it is properly organized. A system of 'credit hours' gives the best scope for a wide variety of skills to be fully utilized in this way and no one can take much advantage – 2 hours cleaning the house for 2 hours repairing the roof seems a fair basis of exchange. The idea may seem far-fatched, but the practicalities are worth exploring – after all society has functioned on a barter system before! The snag, of course, is redress in the case of dissatisfaction. In fact, the law of contract provides for barter, but it could be a complicated business to enforce it. As with most things in life, there is a certain amount of risk but other people would have to take your services on trust too.

Tool Kit

CUTTING

panel saw

tenon saw

Stanley knife

HOLDING

vice

clamps

BORING

awl

DRILLING

hand drill

SMOOTHING

plane

rasp

MEASURING

retractable steel measure
metal rule

try-square

spirit level

WOOD-SHAPING

chisels

JOINING

claw hammer

set of screwdrivers
(to fit both slotted
and cross-headed
screws)

PAINTING

paint brushes

paint rollers

paint pads

glasspaper

wet-and-dry sandpaper

sanding block

PLUMBING

hacksaw

junior hacksaw

file

adjustable spanner

ELECTRICAL

cutters

pliers

wire stripper

insulated screwdriver

neon-tester

Pets

Most households discover sooner or later that animals and children do tend to gravitate towards each other.

Almost all children yearn for a pet at some time or other. They can go off the idea just as quickly, so decide whether *you* want one, since a lot of the responsibility for it is likely to devolve on to you. Pets cost money. Not necessarily in the first instance, since kittens, white mice, budgies, stray dogs and the like are often offered free to good homes. But they have to eat, and there is no National Health Service for animals, though the P.D.S.A. will give emergency treatment free of charge. The larger the animal, the more it will cost to feed, the more space it will occupy and the more potential it will have for doing damage – all points to consider with regard to economy.

A pet is a living creature with needs similar to your own. It requires shelter, suitable living conditions, food and exercise. All of these make demands on the owner. It is manifestly unfair to keep an animal in unsuitable conditions, so consider your circumstances carefully before choosing a pet. Remember that pets need to be looked after, and paid for, when you go on holiday – a kindly neighbour might feed a cat or goldfish, but will not look with favour upon the demands of a six month old puppy or a mature Great Dane. Sometimes a bitch is purchased with the idea of breeding, so that it pays for its keep. If you have no experience, forget this idea. There will be a hefty stud fee, and it costs a lot to feed mother and pups. Complications may arise, which can result in large bills to the vet. The puppies make a lot of extra work and mess, and children will be broken-hearted when you have to sell them.

Fish are the easiest pets of all, though they are unlikely to offer much in the way of affection. White mice, hamsters and gerbils do not cost much to feed, but must be kept clean, or they smell. Guinea pigs are similar, but larger, and consequently eat more. Birds are not much trouble, though you need a suitable cage which can be bought second hand. These are all good 'starter' pets – inexpensive and relatively undemanding. All could be kept in city houses or flats, though guinea pigs are better out of doors.

In the country, or where there is a large garden, tortoises and rabbits are possibilities, but remember if rabbits escape they will wreak havoc in your vegetable garden in no time at all. Rabbits live to eat, and breed. It goes without saying that it is *not* a good idea to bear in mind the breeding aspect with an eye to the stew pot or the freezer if the rabbits are children's pets.

If you want productive pets, hens are worth a try. Find out if local bye-laws and house deeds permit you to keep them; they are not really noisy – the cock is the loud-mouthed one, and you can fortunately dispense with his services as hens lay eggs regardless. Half a dozen hens will not cost much to feed and you might be able to get stale bread or swill cheaply and near at hand. Household scraps can be used but efficient house-keepers should not have many. Hens can make surprisingly intelligent and interesting pets and they do earn their keep in the provision of fresh eggs for most of the year. The mysterious disappearance of one in its old age can usually be successfully stage-managed, especially if you have a freezer, so that the subsequent dinner does not give the show away!

Cats and dogs are perennial favourites. Cats are less trouble as they are much more independent, and they do not require so much food, but it is wise to have them spayed or dressed, according to sex. This, of course, will be an expense. Small dogs are cheaper than large ones to feed and need less exercise. Bitches are more affectionate on the whole, and have less tendency to wander, but unless you are prepared to cope with their twice-yearly period in season a spaying operation will be necessary. Highly bred animals tend to be more delicate – a tough little mongrel could be a more economic choice, but remember that a mongrel puppy whose exact parentage is unknown could turn into almost anything and grow to a prodigious size with an appetite to match. Local cat and dog homes are full of appealing outcasts whose days are numbered unless someone takes them in, and you might find a very suit-able pet there. A nominal charge is made as some kind of insurance that the animal is going to a home where it is really wanted.

Animals in houses make a mess. The larger and hairier they are, the more mess they make. Puppies make puddles – and worse. So do kittens, but they are more quickly trained. Both chew, claw, rip, tear and throw up in inconvenient places. They damage other people's property (and even other people), get fleas, worms, pregnant, ill and into fights. Be aware of all this and the consequent financial implications.

Ponies and donkeys hardly come within the remit of a book on economy, but a goat – if you have the facilities – might just be worth it for the milk! The nanny goat, fortunately, has the lesser tendency to smell.

chapter 12

SIMPLE
ELECTRICITY AND PLUMBING

The mere sound of 'simple electricity and plumbing' may cause your heart to sink to your feet but – unless you have sworn a deliberate oath to get through this life without knowing which end of a screwdriver is the working end – learning how to change a plug, a fuse or a washer will only add to your accomplishments and make life generally less precarious.

Simple electrical procedures

It has to be said: remember always that live electricity in conjunction with water can mean a dead person. Apart from wiring plugs and replacing fuses, leave all other electrical tasks to your Electricity Board or an electrical contractor on the roll of the National Inspection Council for Electrical Installation Contracting – the Electricity Board shops keep such lists.

The first priority on moving into a house is to familiarize yourself with the main fuse boxes and switches. Identify the main switch, circuit switches and fuse box, and label the fuses to save time and temper on that cold, dark night. Keep spare fuse wire, fuses and a torch handy by the main fuse box.

Wiring colour code

A few years ago new colours were adopted for the wires in flexes, and it is essential to know these colour changes. If you are attaching a plug to an appliance which is not new, first check the colours of the wires in the flex of the appliance. The diagrams below show the old and the new colour codes.

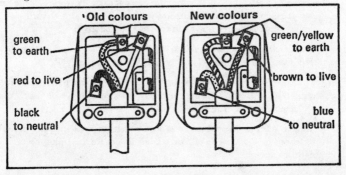

To wire a plug

This is not a difficult task. You will need a small screwdriver and something to cut the wires and unwanted insulation – a proper wire stripper and cutter is better than a pair of nail scissors. An old style 15 amp round pin plug contains no fuse but the wiring procedure is the same as for 13 amp plugs, as shown in the following diagrams.

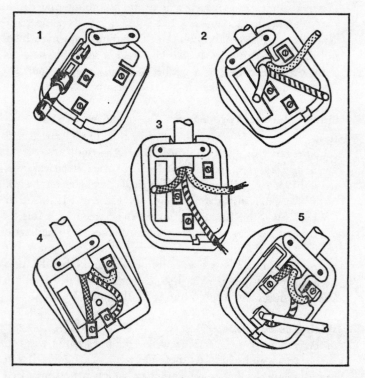

1 Remove cover by loosening screw on underside. Prise out the fuse. Remove one flex clamp screw and loosen the other

2 Cut away about 50 mm (2 in) of the outer sheath. Take care not to cut into the wires. Fix the sheath firmly under the clamp. The wire ends should reach about 13 mm ($\frac{1}{2}$ in) beyond terminals

3 Strip insulation from wire ends to expose 6 mm ($\frac{1}{4}$ in) of wire for screwhole terminals. Allow 13 mm ($\frac{1}{2}$ in) for clamp type terminals

4 Twist the strands of wire and either insert into the holes (screwhole terminals) or loop clockwise round terminals (clamp type). Check that no loose strands of wire remain

5 Tighten screws. Insert the correct fuse to suit the appliance (see p. 142). Re-check that wires are on correct terminals. Replace plug cover and tighten screw

To replace a fuse

A domestic ring main circuit has two types of protection against overloading: a cartridge fuse in the plug protects the appliance; a main fuse in the fuse board protects the circuit. Lighting circuits are protected by a main fuse only. If a fuse keeps on blowing, do not attempt to use a fuse of a higher rating – send for an approved electrician.

Plug fuses (cartridge fuses)

When an appliance refuses to work, switch off both the appliance switch and the socket switch. Remove the plug from the socket, unscrew the top and prise out the fuse. Fit a new fuse (see p.142 for the correct rating) or check the existing fuse as follows: remove the base of a metal torch and connect the suspect fuse between the bottom of the battery and the torch casing. If the bulb does not light up, the fuse has blown. Check the plug terminals for loose connections, replace plug cover and test the appliance again. If it still refuses to work and the main fuse is intact, have it checked by an electrician.

Main fuses

Before checking for a blown main fuse, switch off the main switch which may be on the fuse board or on a separate switch box nearby. Remove and examine each fuse in turn – they may be either cartridge or rewireable type. Check cartridge fuses as described above, and replace as necessary. With a rewireable fuse check for broken wires or scorch marks on the fuse holder. To fit new fuse wire, unscrew the retaining screws and remove the old wire. Wind fuse wire of the correct rating clockwise twice round one terminal and tighten the screw. Route the wire to the other terminal, and again wind round twice clockwise, leaving some slack. Tighten screw, cut off surplus wire.

rewireable main fuses

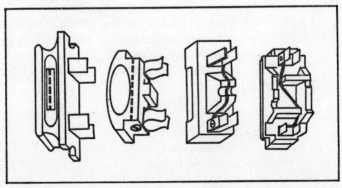

cartridge main fuses

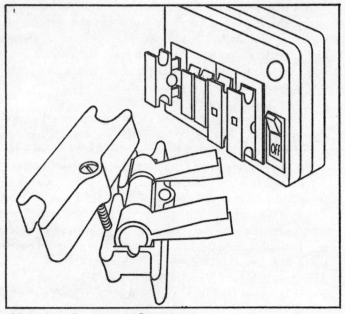

Choosing the correct fuse

Always check that the fuse you fit is of the correct rating for the purpose. Never use a higher rated cartridge fuse or a thicker wire fuse, even as a temporary measure. Never assume that the blown fuse was of the correct rating. Use the following list to guide your choice of fuse. Note: Modern houses may have miniature circuit breakers which are simply reset by pressing a button or switch after the fault has been corrected.

Plug fuses
(Check the rating plate on the base or back of an appliance)

    3 amp – suits appliances rated up to 720 watts.

  13 amp – suits appliances rated between 720 and 3000 watts. Also colour televisions and appliances such as spin driers and vacuum cleaners with electric motors rated at under 720 watts but which take a higher starting current.

Main fuses

     5 amp – lighting circuit
  15/20 amp – immersion heater
  30 amp – ring main circuit
  45 amp – cooker

A guide to running costs

We pay for electricity by the unit. One unit means using electricity at the rate of 1 kilowatt (kW) for 1 hour. The cost per unit is found on an electricity bill, and further information on the various tariffs in operation can be obtained at your local Electricity Board shop. The following is an approximate but handy guide to what you get for **one unit of electricity** around the house.

KITCHEN
    Cooker – daily meals for one
    Dishwasher – dinner dishes for family of four
    Refrigerator – one day's operation
    Tumble drier – 30 minutes' use
    Spin drier – 5 weeks' use in laundry
    Instantaneous water heater – 14 litres (3 gal) hot water
    Vacuum cleaner – 2-3 hours' cleaning
    Extractor fan – 24 hours' use
    Fan heater (2 kW) – 30 minutes' heat
    Food mixer – over 60 cake mixes
    Blender – 280 litres (500 pints) liquid
    Kettle – 7 litres (12 pints) boiling water
    Iron – over 2 hours' use
    Toaster – 70 slices of toast

LIVING AREA
    Radiant heater (3kW) – 20 minutes' heat
    Television: black and white – 7 hours' viewing
                colour – 3 hours' viewing
    Record player – 24 hours' playing
    Light (100 watt) – 10 hours' lighting

BEDROOM
    Convector heater (2 kW) – 30 minutes' heat
    Underblanket – a week's evening use
    Overblanket – 2 full nights' warmth
    Hair drier – 3 hours' use
    Heated rollers – 20 hair-dos
    Lamp (60 watt) – $16\frac{1}{2}$ hours' use

BATHROOM
    Towel rail (250 watt) – 4 hours' operation
    Infra-red heater (1 kW) 1 hour's heat

GARAGE/WORK AREA
Power drill – 2-3 hours' use
Battery charger – 30 hours' charging

LARGER APPLIANCES
Washing machine: automatic – 9 units for weekly wash for
　　　　　　family of four
twin tub – 12 units for weekly wash for family of four
　　　　　　including electrical water-heating
Freezer – 1½ units per 28 litres (1 cubic foot) per week
Hot water – (if tank is well-lagged) 85 units for family of four
　　　　　　per week
Shower – 10 units for a shower a day for a week

How to read your meter
This is quite a simple task and essential if you wish to keep
records of your electricity consumption for reasons of economy.
There are basically two kinds of meter – digital and dial.

Digital meter
This is the modern type with the number of units shown by a
simple row of figures. The special White Meter shows two
digital indicators – one for lower cost night rate electricity, the
other for day rate.

The reading on the digital meter is the total number of units
used since installation of the meter. Subtract your previous
reading from the new reading to find your consumption.

Dial meter
When reading a dial meter, remember that adjacent dials
revolve in opposite directions (see diagram p. 145). Ignore the
dial marked $\frac{1}{10}$ as it is there only for testing purposes. Start by
reading the dial showing single units, then read the dial showing
tens of units, then the one showing hundreds, then thousands,
then tens of thousands. Work from right to left and write the
figures down in that order.

Always write down the number the pointer has *passed*. If the
pointer is anywhere between, say 3 and 4, write down 3. If the
pointer is directly over a figure, say 7, look at the pointer on
the dial immediately to the right. If this pointer is between 9
and 0, write down 6. If, however, this pointer is between 0 and
1, write down 7. As with the digital meter, subtract a new
reading from the previous reading to find the number of units
of electricity used.

Sample dial meter reading
Read from right to left 1-5

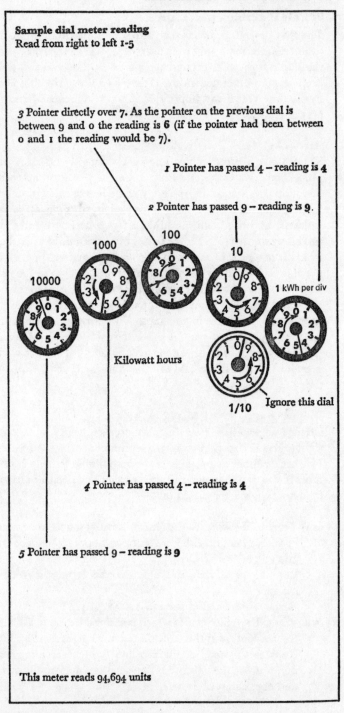

3 Pointer directly over 7. As the pointer on the previous dial is between 9 and 0 the reading is **6** (if the pointer had been between 0 and 1 the reading would be 7).

1 Pointer has passed 4 – reading is **4**

2 Pointer has passed 9 – reading is **9**.

100

1000

10

10000

1 kWh per div

Kilowatt hours

1/10

Ignore this dial

4 Pointer has passed 4 – reading is **4**

5 Pointer has passed 9 – reading is **9**

This meter reads 94,694 units

Simple plumbing procedures

The first procedure in moving into a house is to find out the location of the main stop-cock and to discover the purpose of all the other stop-cocks around the house so that you are well-prepared if a hitch does occur. There could be a sizeable flood in the time you spend hunting around for a means of cutting off the supply.

Air locks

These make their presence known by banging noises in the pipes. Some water systems have a tendency to form air locks, and if this is a persistent problem you are best to call a plumber. Sometimes a minor air lock is caused by turning off a tap suddenly and hard. This is quite easily treated by turning the tap on again then closing the water off more gently. A bad air lock will cause a cessation of the flow altogether. It may be possible to clear it by fixing a short length of hose to the cold water tap in the kitchen. Fit the other end of the hose to the hot tap – you will need what are known as jubilee clips to keep the hose firmly attached to the taps. Now turn on the hot tap followed by the cold and let the water run for a few seconds. (You are trying to clear the air lock by using the mains water pressure.) Turn off the cold tap first and then turn off the hot tap.

Dripping tap

Change the washer (see diagram opposite). First obtain the right type and size of washer from a plumber or hardware store. Synthetic rubber or nylon is best and suitable for hot or cold taps. If you can only get a rubber washer you need a hard one for a hot tap, soft for a cold tap.

1 Turn off the water at the mains, also any source of heating. (You need not do either if you have 'Supataps'.) Open tap and run off water.
2 Remove tap cover and unscrew the large nut with a spanner.
3 Remove the head of the tap.
4 You will see the washer which is secured by a nut. Change the washer, with the maker's name facing upwards.
5 Replace the head of the tap and tighten the large nut. Screw down the tap cover. Turn on the water supply again and check that all is well.

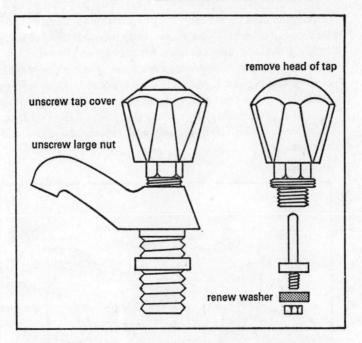

unscrew tap cover

unscrew large nut

remove head of tap

renew washer

Burst pipes

Turn off the main stop-cock, cold water cistern valve, if fitted, and any source of water heating. Prevent water spreading by plugging the burst with tightly wrapped rags. Place a bucket below the leak. Turn on hot and cold taps, unless you know which system has the burst. Fetch a plumber as soon as possible.

WC cistern overflow

This may be caused by a jammed or perforated ball-cock. The first is simply a case of clearing the jam, which sometimes occurs if the mechanism has not been used for some time and a gentle wiggle will do the trick. If it keeps recurring further investigation will be required. A perforated ball-cock will be partially sunk owing to the weight of water inside it, and this is why the water keeps flowing instead of turning off. Remove the float by unscrewing it, empty it of water and then screw it back on again. Make a temporary repair by wrapping the ball in a polythene bag and tying this tightly round the lever. Replace the leaking ball as soon as possible – it screws on quite simply.

Another cause of overflow may be a faulty washer in the ball valve (see diagram). To renew this, take out the split pin holding the lever arm and unscrew the cap on the valve case. Push out the piston and unscrew the two parts, prise out the washer and replace it with a new one. Some modern cisterns have the more simple arrangement of a diaphragm operating against a nylon nozzle. To replace this unscrew the cap at the valve end of the lever, remove and replace the worn diaphragm.

Ball Valve

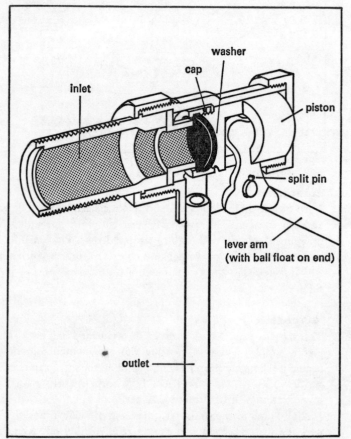

If you feel that these undertakings are too complicated you can either turn off the water supply at the cistern stop-cock, or tie up the ball-cock to a piece of wood resting across the top of the cistern. Seek help, but it need not be professional if you also have a skill to trade (see p. 135).

chapter 13

THE GARDEN

A garden may, or may not be 'a lovesome thing', but a plot of productive ground can certainly save you money. A well-tilled plot of about 100 square metres (120 square yards) should keep 3-6 people well supplied with vegetables for most of the year. It does need careful planning of sowing and planting, and it can't all be done for free.

Garden tools
Seeds cost money, so do tools, although you do not need a great many – a spade, rake, hoe, fork and trowel would suffice. Most people who have gardens will already own these, of course, but if you are a flat dweller lucky enough to have secured an allotment or share of a garden, it is as well to have some idea of what your financial outlay is likely to be. Where several people work adjoining allotments a certain amount of sharing is possible, especially with more expensive items like wheelbarrows.

Compromise
If you already own a garden, take a closer look at it. Beds of flowers and roses are unquestionably attractive, but you cannot make a salad of roses or pop a crocus in the soup. A large extent of lawn requires mowing, and the only diet provided is one suitable for rabbits or sheep, though the mowings can certainly be usefully recycled on the compost heap. Compromise is the answer. Reduce the lawn and the flower areas and plant fruit and vegetables instead, and remember the one golden rule for successful gardening – *what you take out you must replace*. Starved soil will not furnish you with good crops of vegetables. There must be plenty of organic matter in the soil, in the form of farmyard manure (if you can get it) or compost (make your own). Buying commercially prepared fertilizer is expensive, so use alternatives where possible.

Home-made compost heap
Almost anything which will rot down can go on the compost

heap. Vegetable waste, garden waste, mowings, leaves, clippings, weeds, vacuum cleaner dust, wool, hair and fluff, soot, feathers, rags, bones, ashes and torn-up newspaper are all suitable. Avoid food scraps – they encourage mice, rats, cats and dogs. You can buy a special container but, as usual, it is cheaper to construct something yourself. As long as air can enter at the bottom and sides and the contents are kept within bounds, protected from wind and predators, nature will do the rest. It does help things along if you add a little compost activator from time to time. The whole process takes several months, so it is a good idea to have two heaps – one to use and one in construction.

Plants from seed

Grow your own plants from seed. You don't need a greenhouse, a sunny windowsill will do for getting things started indoors. Polythene bags and margarine cartons are almost as good as a propagating frame, but it is worth spending some money on a good seed compost to give your little plants a flying start. It is sterilized so there is less chance of disease. Nothing is more depressing than the sight of promising seedlings shrivelling up or keeling over. Cloches made of strong wire and polythene will get plants started off early out of doors, as they help warm up the soil and give protection from frost and cold winds. Cold frames are not difficult to construct from scrap wood and glass or heavy polythene. Old windows are better still. See if the local joiner has any which have been removed from houses because of rot around the frames – this won't matter for your purpose.

Vegetables

Find out from local gardeners what grows well in your area. Do not waste money and energy trying to grow a crop which is unsuitable for your soil. Potatoes, onions and lettuce will grow almost anywhere. Carrots need care because of carrot fly which can devastate an entire crop in a few days. Green vegetables like cauliflower, cabbage, peas and beans tend to produce a glut at the same time. This is fine if you have a freezer (and time to cope!) but it is difficult for an amateur to slow down or speed up crops like these in order to obtain a steady supply. Leeks and Brussels sprouts are obliging in this respect, and useful in the winter months. Courgettes, also known as zucchini or baby marrows, are really easy to grow and will keep you supplied for months in summer (they freeze well, too). To get the best results, bring the seeds on indoors. Individual peat pots are worth the money for this crop, as they do not respond well to being tipped out and replanted. Peat pots eliminate the need for this, as the roots grow through the pot which will eventually break down, and you will recoup the cost of the pots with your first half dozen courgettes. When the young plants have been hardened off in the cold frame for a week or two, plant them out in a really heavily manured bed and keep them well-watered. The resultant crop will astound you.

Root vegetables can be stored in a cool, dark place which is dry and well-ventilated. Carrots are best buried in clean sand. Dry off onions and string them up in an airy shed.

Fruit

Trees take up space, and they also take some time to mature and produce crops. Bushes are a good investment, and raspberries, gooseberries, black and red currants are all easy to grow. Strawberries can be grown in tubs, pots, barrels or window boxes with surprising success, but they need plenty of feeding and watering in a more restricted environment. Nevertheless, they become a distinct possibility for city dwellers who only have a small space or terrace out of doors. A beer barrel will grow a lot of strawberries, and the flowers and foliage are decorative – the latter turns a beautiful shade of red in autumn. Tomatoes will grow on a sunny windowsill or in a porch, and even outdoors in sunny sheltered spots.

Rhubarb is easiest of all and grows in spite of everything. Feed it well and force it in early spring by covering it with cloches, glass, a bottomless old bucket or dustbin.

All fruit can be frozen, bottled or made into jam, which makes for savings in the housekeeping budget. Keep all your small empty jars for the extra jam – it never comes out in exact weights – and store these for Christmas presents. Four mini pots make an ideal gift, especially for those living alone.

Herbs

Fresh herbs add interest and variety to the plainest of food, and casseroles made with cheaper cuts of meat acquire a real gourmet flavour when herbs are added. Dried herbs are expensive and pale into insignificance beside their fresh counterparts which are easy to grow in pots on the windowsill.

They will do even better out of doors of course, but those without gardens have a chance of another small horticultural venture here. Most herbs can be cultivated from seed – you will get dozens more than you need, so plant some extra ones in painted cream cartons (make a few holes in the bottom for drainage) and these will make useful and welcome gifts for friends. Parsley, chives, different kinds of mint, lemon balm, thyme, sage and marjoram all grow very easily and would make a good start. You can branch out with basil, rosemary dill, tarragon, fennel and a host of others if you also have the space, taste and enthusiasm.

Pooling resources

Flowers are, for most of us, an essential part of the garden, and borders of your favourites can front a vegetable patch, but don't overlook the decorative value of fruit trees and bushes. There is no real need to separate the flowers and vegetables. Combine the best of both worlds. Pool resources with other gardeners too, and swop any surplus plants. Learn to take cuttings – all you need is a sharp knife, a cream carton with good sowing compost and a polythene bag. Hormone rooting powder helps, but is by no means essential. A healthy cutting fresh from a neighbour's garden will do just as well, and perhaps better, than expensive nursery stock. You must have patience to be a gardener – and a considerable amount of fortitude in the face of the climate!

Improvise

Many garden requisites can be improvised cheaply. It is far too easy to *buy* just what you need instead of looking around for no-cost alternatives. Never throw away polythene – small bags are useful for propagating. Large pieces can be nailed to wood to cover a cold frame or used with wire to make cloches. Black polythene is excellent for covering the compost heap, or for protecting plants, or using in place of straw for strawberries. If you do use straw, put it on the compost heap when the berry crop is finished. Plastic cartons make useful pots for seeds and cuttings.

Pests

Plastic cartons also make effective traps for earwigs. Stuff a little dead grass or straw inside and place them upside down on canes in the garden. The earwig is apparently very pleased to make its home there, and you then have the gruesome task of exterminating the inhabitants. There are other gruesome tasks in the garden. Slugs, snails, millipedes and greenfly (with its black and white cousins) are the chief enemies. Clensel makes a relatively cheap and efficient plant spray, has the merit of being safe and also has other uses in the home.

To keep down slugs, you will have to buy slug bait, but do not use it to broadcast. Place a few pieces below a piece of slate or a flat stone and the slugs will find it. It is better to renew bait frequently rather than waste a lot in one night. There are various species of slug; huge black fat ones and smaller grey slimy ones (ugh!) but the ones which do most damage are the little black 'keel' slugs which live in the soil and come out at night.

Shop carefully when you go to buy proprietary garden aids. Compare prices and read labels – often one product will do more than one thing – choose general purpose products whenever possible. If it kills seven pests and you have only two of them, you will doubtless acquire some of the others before the season is out, but there is also the useful point that their arrival may be thwarted.

Country finds

Home-made compost has already been mentioned, but leaf mould from oak or beech trees is another useful addition to the soil especially if it is of heavy clay. Leaf mould may be readily available to country dwellers but it is quite easy to gather a few carrier bagfuls on a country walk or picnic. At the same time look out for dead brushwood which makes a good twiggy support for peas and beans (you could also grow your own bamboo canes). Remember that you must be able to transport your spoils – a dead spruce tree will not be welcomed on the local bus!

Protection from birds

Fruit needs protection from birds, and you can buy plastic net for this purpose, but if you have a chance to visit a fishing port you may be able to pick up an old fishing net very cheaply. A few repairs might be necessary, but it will last for years. Old jam jars placed on their sides make a good protection for strawberries and also hasten the ripening if you want a few early ones, but this is hardly a practical proposition for the whole crop.

Protection from light fingers

Protecting your crops from human predators is another matter and those who have allotments encounter a difficult problem which may be best tackled on a collective basis. Community effort may make it possible to organize stouter and more effective fencing or to arrange a watch system based on shifts during the picking season.

A garden beside the house is safer, especially if the boundary fencing also serves as a screen to conceal what is growing in the way of crops. A dog is often a useful deterrent to unwelcome intruders – a fictitious notice 'beware of the dog' may even dissuade an intruder who fears either the 'dog' or its clamour!

chapter 14

CONSUMER PROTECTION

As a consumer of goods and services you have certain rights. The more straitened your finances, the more important are these rights. But many people forget that consumers also have responsibilities – there are two parties to a bargain!

Money can be wasted on bad buys, and bad buys are as often due to uninformed shoppers as uninformed shopkeepers. Buying and selling today is a cut-throat business. Advertising, competition, discount houses, special offers and manufacturers' recommended prices leave the unfortunate consumer totally bewildered and at a loss to know where to turn for the best buy. The final choice of what to buy (or indeed *whether* to buy at all) is entirely up to you, but the better informed you are beforehand, the wiser your choice is likely to be.

Sources of information

It is your responsibility to be in possession of all the necessary information, and the sources are many and varied.

1 *Friends* who already possess the article you want to buy. Consider, in the cold light of day, whether you are trying to convince yourself of need on the basis of keeping up with the Joneses. Friends' opinions may be biased for or against, so seek further objective advice.

2 *Advertisements and manufacturers' leaflets* are likely to be biased also, since they are all trying to convince you that their product is best. Nevertheless they usually have useful factual information about the product.

3 *Newspaper and magazine articles* should be less biased unless the journalist has a particular enthusiasm for a certain brand. Some magazines run a regular consumer feature and these are a good source of information, although you will be lucky to find a particular topic just when you want it.

4 *Radio and television programmes* Shopping advice is usually sound. Consumer programmes, especially on television, tend to concentrate on entertainment value rather than useful information – which is a pity, but understandable.

5 *The Consumers' Association*, publishers of *Which?* magazine. You have to become a subscriber to obtain *Which?* but it should be possible to borrow a copy for reference. All their information is available at your nearest Consumer Advice Centre.

6 *Consumer Advice Centres* are now appearing in High Streets all over the UK and do NOT exist solely to deal with complaints. They would much rather help you to buy the right article than sort out the mess after you have bought – or been sold! – the wrong one. Pre-purchase counselling is an important part of their service and they can give you up-to-date information more easily and quickly than you will get anywhere else. You will be helped to establish your own needs and then a suitable range of products will be suggested. The final choice is left to you, but this service is particularly valuable when you want to make a major purchase, for example, of expensive electrical equipment. Their weekly food price surveys are worth noting also – you may save up to 10% of your weekly shopping bill.

7 *Advice in the shop* Once upon a time, this was wholly reliable. Small shopkeepers wished to keep their customers and did this by satisfying them (here writes a small shopkeeper's daughter!). Happily, you can still get good advice but it is much less easy to come by. Shops have grown bigger and more impersonal; staff turnover is rapid, and though responsible managers do their best, through staff training, to keep their assistants well-informed, the task is well nigh impossible. A rapidly changing market based on constantly developing technology does not help, either. There are far too many products for any one person to be knowledgeable about them all. If you can find a shop where you are a valued customer, stick with it! Such service may cost you more, but it could be worth it in the long run.

8 *Labelling* Informative labelling gives guidance about standards, safety, composition and care. Here are a few of the main care and advice labels you will encounter. More are appearing all the time – look out for them. (See also p. 69.)

1 British Standards Institution
Kitemark

Appears on goods which have been made to comply with standards laid down by the Institution. British Standards are documents which set out the requirements necessary to ensure that goods are fit for the purpose for which they are intended. Tests are continually carried out after the Kitemark has been awarded. It can be seen on over 200 different products, including crash helmets, car safety belts, oil heaters, locks, pressure cookers, plastic goods and hand tools.

2 British Electro-Technical Approvals Board

Their mark appears on tested electrical goods which have passed minimum safety requirements, as set out in a British Standard. Safety requirements have been laid down for the majority of domestic electrical appliances and the mark is your assurance that the product has been passed as electrically safe.

3 British Gas

The nationalized gas industry runs a 'Seal of Service' scheme for gas appliances sold in its own showrooms or by authorized dealers. Such appliances have passed British Gas standards for performance, reliability and fitness for purpose.

9 *Codes of practice* are drawn up by trade associations for their member firms. These voluntary codes are designed to improve traders' standards of service to customers, though they give no extra right in law. You will usually see the trade association symbol displayed on the premises.

10 *Consumer groups* are pressure groups formed to pursue the interests and/or complaints of consumers. Find out if you have one locally.

Think and enquire *before* you buy. Ask yourself what you need, what you can afford, and what functions you want the product to perform. When you have satisfactory answers to these questions, make use of some of the foregoing sources of information, and you should be assured of successful shopping.

Shoppers' rights

You are entitled under the Sale of Goods Act amended by the Supply of Goods (Implied Terms) Act 1973 to:

1 Goods which are of merchantable quality – an iron should work when it is plugged in; a sheet should not have a hole in the centre of it. (The price of the goods has a certain relevance here – a cheap article will not be of such *high* merchantable quality as a more expensive one).

2 Goods fit for the purpose for which they would normally be used – a kettle should not leak; carpet dye should not come off on clothes.

3 Goods which meet the description applied to them – a 2-litre pan must hold two litres; a package labelled 'one pair blue pillowcases' should not contain white ones.

If any of these obligations are not met the retailer has broken the contract and you may be entitled to your money back.

How to complain

Should you have a complaint, return the goods to the shop where you bought them, taking with you any bill or receipt. It is not easy to complain, but remember you are not begging a favour. Ask for someone responsible, act reasonably and keep your temper. There is nothing to be gained by behaving aggressively, even if the 'other side' becomes somewhat heated!

You can also write a letter of complaint but always keep a copy of the letter, and send only copies of receipts. Wait until you are in a calm frame of mind before writing and stick to the facts. Type your letter if possible.

Should you decide to telephone about a complaint be sure to get the name of the person who deals with your enquiry as this will save time in any subsequent telephone calls.

Redress

If your complaint is justified the shopkeeper may offer to replace or repair the article and this may be a satisfactory solution. In certain cases you have the right to your money back, but only when you have acted immediately and the goods have been hardly used. You are also entitled to redress if you have suffered loss or damage as a result of faulty goods. You are *not* obliged to accept a credit note, but if you do you will not be able to claim money at a later date – only goods to the same value.

Most complaints are settled reasonably provided they are justified, and shopkeepers mindful of goodwill may replace articles when they are not legally obliged to do so.

Expert help

When you fail to get satisfaction for a complaint which you feel is genuine, the best thing to do is seek expert help, and there are three places where you can get it: your local Citizens' Advice Bureau; the nearest Consumer Advice Centre (it may be a mobile caravan which visits your district regularly); and the Trading Standards or Consumer Protection Department of your local authority. There are many more bodies who can help, but any of these three will be able to put you on the right track and help to ensure fair play all round. The customer is not always right, but he or she does stand a good chance of having genuine claims of complaint settled. Sometimes it may be necessary to go to law, but be guided by the experts. It is unwise and potentially very expensive to pursue a claim against their advice.

Metrication

If you haven't been to school within the past ten years or so, you will probably feel queasy at the mere mention of metrication – since it won't just disappear, the following points and handy conversions are provided for easy reference until the day when you finally become converted.

Metric aids

The first aid is a metric tape measure which also has imperial markings – but try not to look at the inches and get accustomed to your new bust size of around 90!

In the kitchen, a set of metric measuring spoons will prove very useful, but the plastic 5 ml spoon supplied by the chemist when he dispenses medicine is better than nothing. Another invaluable aid is a measuring jug marked with both metric and imperial quantities. And a kitchen scale with both sets of measures will make a good investment against the day when recipes are wholly metric. (Both measuring jugs and scales can be bought metric only.)

The jingles below were given out by the Metrication Board. They are easy to learn by heart and make useful reminders when shopping.

Two and a quarter pounds of jam
Weigh about a kilogram

ounces	grammes	pounds	kilograms
1	30	1	$\frac{1}{2}$
2	55	2	1
4	115	3	$1\frac{1}{2}$
6	170		
8	225		
10	285		
12	340	(The tables give approximate	
16	455	but handy conversions)	

A litre of water's
A pint and three quarters

fluid ounces	millilitres
1	25
2	50
5 (¼ pint)	150
10 (½ pint)	300
15 (¾ pint)	400
20 (1 pint)	600
35	1 litre

A metre measures three foot three
It's longer than a yard you see

Fabric lengths are sold by the metre to the nearest 10 cm (4 in).
Fabric widths are as follows:

inches	centimetres
27	70
35/36	90
44/45	115
48	120
54/56	140
60	150

Metric beds

	width	length
Small single	90 cm	190 cm
Standard single	100 cm	200 cm
Small double	135 cm	190 cm
Standard double	150 cm	200 cm

Bunk bed sizes are the same as before (2'6" x 6'3") but are now
described as 75 cm × 190 cm.

Room heating
For central heating, temperatures are usually
Bedroom 18°C
Living room: 22°C

INDEX

fuse: box 139; cartridge 141, *142*; main 141, 142; plug 141, 142; rating 141, 142; rewireable 141, *141*; to replace 141; wire 139, 141

Garden 46, 149–54; furniture 32, 34; tools 149
gas 15, 129; cookers 42; Seal of Service *156*, 157
glass 130–1; to clean 131
glass fibre 55; to wash 82–3
gloves 94, 100, 113, 114
glycerine 89
grass stain 91
grate 129, 130
gravy stain 86, 91
grease stain 88, 91, 93
grill: double 42–3; infra-red 48
group purchase 13, 47
guarantee 39, 51
gutters 134

Hair lacquer, to remove 133
hand washing 45, 72, 77
hardboard 23
hard floors: care of 27; coverings 22; to patch 27
hard water 73, 125
hats, to clean 112–13
haybox 49
H cowl 130
heat loss 127
heat marks, to remove 38
heat, to conserve 127–30
heatspots 132
heavy duty wash product 72, 87
hems 64, 121
hens, to keep 138
herbs 151–2
hire purchase 10, 17, 41
HLCC 68, 69, 70
hotplates 42, 128
housekeeping 11
hydrogen peroxide 87, 88, 133
hygiene, personal 133

Immersion heater 128
inflation 10
infra-red grill 48
ink stains 31, 88, 91
instructions 37, 50–1
insulation 126, 127
insurance 7–8, 47, 51, 52
interest, true rate 17
ironing 54, 56, 79–81, 84; curtains 66, 82; glaze 80

iron-on patches 116–18, 121
irons 49, 80, 111, 143

Jam 11, 151
jumble 10; sales 60, 66–7, 95, 105
junk 10; shops 40
jute 21

Kettle 128, 131, 143
Kitemark 34, *156*, 157
knitting 106; machine 106; wool 126
knitwear to wash 83

Lagging 126, 128
lampshades 65, 99
launderette 45, 77, 81, 82, 95; dyeing 97; tumble drier 84
leaf mould 153
leather: to clean 31, 109, 110, 113–14; to wash 113
letter box 127
light bulbs 49–50, 129
light duty wash product 72–3, 82, 84
linen 54; bed 33, 55–9, 77; cupboard 66; dyeing 95; ironing 81; seconds 66; storage 66; table 60–1, 67; using up 125; washing 77, 81
lining, curtain 62, 64–5
lino 20, 22, 23, 27, 37, 126; care of 27; paint 28; patching 27; polish 27; seals 27; second-hand 28; tiles 22, 27
loose covers 65; washing 83
loss leader 11
low-lather powder 72
lubricants 89

Machine washing 78
mail order 39, 53
maintenance 11, 133–4
make-up stain 91
man-made fibres: carpets 20–1; dyeing 95, 97; ironing 80; loose covers 65; re-using 107; soft furnishing 54–5; solvents 88; starch 75; washing 68–79, 81; wearing quality 103
mattress: foam 34; spring interior 33–4
meter, to read 144, *145*
methylated spirit 86, 88, 133
metrication 159–60
mildew 79, 91; carpets 24; knitwear 83; linen 66